Women and Creativity

Joelynn Snyder-Ott

Les Femmes Publishing
Millbrae, California

Cover design: Betsy Bruno

Copyright © 1978 by Les Femmes Publishing

Les Femmes Publishing
231 Adrian Road
Millbrae, California 94030

First Printing, January, 1978

Made in the United States of America

Library of Congress Cataloging in Publication Data

Snyder-Ott, Joelynn, 1940-
    Women and Creativity.

    Includes bibliographical references
    CONTENTS: The female experience and artistic creativity.—A woman's place is in the home.—Creativity/pro-creativity (tackling the next taboo). [etc.]
    1. Women artists.   2. Women in art.   I. Title.
N8354.S64   700   77-77954
ISBN 0-89087-989-3

1   2   3   4   5   6   7   8—84 83 82 81 80 79 78

iv

Contents

Introduction   ix

The Female Experience   1
   and Artistic Creativity

Female Iconography   13
   at Stonehenge

A View from England   23

Women in Art   27

A Woman's Place   43

Art as Yin in a   53
   Yang Society

Angelica Kauffman: 69
   Rival to Gainsborough

500 Years of Birth   83
   in Art Forms—No One
   Gives a Damn!

Dialogue with a Craftswoman   99

Creativity—Procreativity   109

An Art School for Women   119

Feminist Art Programs   131

Bibliography   143

DEDICATION

To my daughter, Lee Shaun, who has enriched my life,
remaining always my *joie de vivre.*

Acknowledgments

I would like to thank the National Art Education Association for granting permission to publish "A Female Experience and Artistic Creativity" from Art Education, Volume 27/Number 6, September, 1974; Cindy Nemser, editor of The Feminist Art Journal for granting permission to publish "A Woman's Place," originally published under the title "A Woman's Place is in the Home (that she built)," September, 1974; The Moore College of Art Alumnae Association for permission to publish "A View from England," originally titled "A Feminist Artist in England (through a class darkly)," March, 1976. I would also like to acknowledge the museums, private collectors, and artists who granted me permission to publish reproductions of art work from their respective collections. Thanks also to the Ryerson Library of the Chicago Institute of Art, Chicago, Illinois; The Courtauld Institute of Art Library, University of London, England; His Grace, the Duke of Northumberland of Syon House and Alnwick Castle, England—a special thank you for permitting me access to their libraries and collections respectively. Acknowledgment is also extended to Ms. Jean Smith, Arts

Librarian at the Pennsylvania State University, University Park, Pennsylvania. Thank you to Robert W. Ott, who so kindly took many of the necessary photographs. A special thanks to Ruth Kramer, publisher, who enthusiastically supported this effort, and my editor, David Morris, and editorial assistant, Gail Hynes.

And lastly, but perhaps most importantly, to my parents, Richard Lee and Gertrude W. Yungel Snyder, who have encouraged me unselfishly to strive for and fully use my creative energies towards expressing myself as a total human being, regardless of society's sex-oriented stereotypes. To them, the biggest thanks of all, with love.

Joelynn Snyder-Ott

Introduction

This book began to take form back in 1972 when I was returning from a gallery in New York City on what I thought would be a very long and boring bus ride. I had picked up a copy of a new magazine entitled *The New Woman* and was casually paging through it when I came to an article interviewing two women artists, women in fact who would later become very well-known as feminist artists and leaders — Judy Chicago and Miriam Shapiro. To my amazement, I found their statements reinforced what I, too, had felt about women in art and "female imagery" but my ideas had only been thought and never expressed for fear I would be ridiculed. Here however, was an article that expressed in no uncertain terms the very ideas that I was too timid to even mumble about. Before the long bus ride ended, I had rethought my own attitudes toward my women art students, my own work, what I had been "taught" in art history classes.

Naturally, the seed of this heightened awareness concerning women's contributions had been germinating for quite some time and it wasn't just this one article that did it, but nevertheless, I felt a camaraderie with these two feminist sister artists and their statements. In the next few days I went to our university library to obtain some material on past women artists, and found, to my amazement, only huge volumes of male artists' work. Women's contributions were usually buried between huge chapters of male artists' work, or shelved in the back stacking areas in dusty volumes.

This book then is a documentation of my experiences as an artist, teacher, and what I later found myself becoming— a researcher of women's art. If the words in this book reveal even a few of the baffling experiences and secrets women artists are exposed to and unconsciously incorporate, and if this in turn gives a heightened awareness of women artists, then this book will have served its purpose.

To the many women artists and art students who shared their thoughts, experiences, and emotions, I give my thanks. For women everywhere, the women artists in this book have set a precedent and will continue to serve as positive role models for our future generations. We as women must never again allow the dust to gather on our contributions to Western civilization.

But it is obvious that the values of women differ very often from the values which have been made by the other sex; naturally this is so. Yet it is the masculine values that prevail. Speaking crudely, football and sport are "important"; the worship of fashion, the buying of clothes "trivial." And these values are inevitably transferred from life to fiction. This is an important book, the critic assumes, because it deals with war. This is an insignificant book because it deals with the feelings of women in a drawing-room. A scene in a battlefield is more important than a scene in a shop—everywhere and much more subtly the difference of value persists. The whole structure, therefore, of the early nineteenth-century novel was raised, if one was a woman, by a mind which was slightly pulled from the straight, and made to alter its clear vision in deference to external authority. One has only to skim those old forgotten novels and listen to the tone of voice in which they are written to divine that the writer was meeting criticism; she was saying this by way of aggression, or that by way of conciliation. She was admitting that she was "only a woman," or protesting that she was "as good as a man." She met that criticism as her temperament dictated, with docility and diffidence, or with anger and emphasis. It does not matter which it was; she was thinking of something other than the thing itself. Down comes her book upon our heads. There was a flaw in the centre of it. And I thought of all the women's novels that lie scattered, like small pock-marked apples in an orchard, about the secondhand book shops of London. It was the flaw in the centre that had rotted them. She had altered her values in deference to the opinion of others.

The Female
Experience and
Artistic Creativity

The arts of a society mirror man's values and attitudes, but what about women's values and attitudes? Western civilization's culture and arts are *male*-dominated and *male*-oriented. Women's highest artistic achievements are off the scene, seldom heard, or if heard, devalued, and finally viewed, but not observed. If you doubt this, there is a simple test: Name just five women artists and their contributions to history.

What is the "female experience"? Why distinguish between male and female experience? You might argue that one creates as an individual regardless of sex. However, we know the sum total of our experiences reflects in our individual statements as artists, but as women artists we have been forced to see the world, ourselves, and other women as men see us. Simply because we as women still believe our experiences, as Virginia Woolf states in the prologue, are "trivial"!

1

The "male perception" has become accepted as the "universal vision." At one time, I too believed that being referred to as a "woman" artist was an unjustified prefix to place before my name. As a woman art student I had always had great confidence in what was *male*. I sought male approval for my work. As a woman I believed that being told that I painted "like a man" or "thought like a man" was the ultimate compliment and goal. Even semantics became important to me concerning my exhibitions. My exhibits were carefully listed as "one-man." There was always the possibility that someone wouldn't take my work (or me) seriously if the prefix "woman" were attached to my name. This of course was not an unfounded fear. An example of this sexism can be documented in the following review concerning the work of the great living sculptor Louise Nevelson. This review appeared in *Cue Magazine* October 4, 1941:

> We learned the artist is a woman, in time to check our enthusiasm. Had it been otherwise we might have hailed these sculptural expressions as by surely a great figure among moderns. See them by all means—painted plaster figures and continuous line drawing that take much knowledge from Picasso and Ozenfant and from Mayan and Indian expressions. I suspect that the artist is clowning—but with what excellent equipment artistically.

So, if I was not to be taken seriously either, because I was a woman, I concluded that I would disguise my sex. I internalized the male value structure as well. My work became eclectically *male*, influenced as it were by male artists. I truly believed that if I succeeded as an artist, it would have to be in spite of my sex. I hoped that I would have the stamina to become one of those courageous women in history who broke with convention and dared to use her talent and intellect. I had a rude awakening.

Marcia Tucker, an associate curator of the Whitney Museum, stated in an article appearing in *Ms* Magazine entitled "By-Passing the Gallery System," that of ten leading New York galleries, 96.4 percent of their artists are male. The Guggenheim Museum has had no major woman's exhibit, and the Museum of Modern Art had four shows by women between 1942 and 1969.

We can change this situation. Naturally, the first step in solving the problem is an awareness and acceptance that it does exist. Secondly, we must become knowledgeable concerning women's contributions in the arts. By education we will destroy the stereotype that artists are always of the male gender. This education will have a long-reaching effect on future generations of museum directors, art educators, curators, and most importantly, the future art patrons and collectors. We must encourage research concerning women's contributions. Libraries today carry a limited number of books dealing with women's contributions, and even fewer visual examples of their work such as slides or posters. I have found that women's historical contributions have been buried so well that I sometimes feel like an archaeologist, crying out in delight (to the annoyance of the librarian) as I "excavate" some small reference to a woman painter or architect such as Elizabeth Vigée-Lebrun or Angelica Kauffman buried or wedged in between page-long articles and huge color reproductions of male artists' work.

Where do we begin? Elizabeth Gould Davis, in her book *The First Sex*, states

> According to mythology women are given credit for inventing the flute, chariot, wheel, ship, art of numbers, fire, cooking, weaving and spinning. In other words women invented ceramics, agriculture, land transportation, animal domestication, commerce, math, handicrafts, domestic economy, and industry.

In addition, in certain cultures all the art is and was made by women. All Navaho blankets are woven by women; almost all American basketry and pottery is done by women. The huts of the Australian, the black camel hair tents of the Bedouin, the yurta of the nomads of Central Asia, the earth lodges of the Omaha, and the pueblos of the Hopi were all the exclusive work of women.

If we search diligently we may discover an extensive contribution by women in the fine arts also. In the 16th century there was a painter named Sonfonisba Anguissola who was most famous for her portraits. The 16th century also recorded Catherine Van Hemessen, a painter whose patron was the Queen of Hungary. Van Hemessen was also listed by her married name "Sanders" and was most famous as a miniaturist. Artemisia Gentileschi, a 17th century Italian, was trained by her father who was also a painter. His paintings are represented in several school poster art reproductions, but unfortunately her work is not. Judith Leyster, who lived from 1609 to 1660, became a pupil of Frans Hals in Haarlem. Many of her paintings have been attributed to the Dutch painter (Hals)—something that happened to other women in history as well. There was Rosalba Carriera, a 17th century painter. Angelica Kauffman, born in 1741 in Switzerland, was a founding member of the Royal Academy in England. Elizabeth-Vigée Lebrun, a French 18th century painter, was a favorite painter of Marie-Antoinette, and painted at least twenty versions of the Queen and her children. She was a great favorite at the French court, and after the French Revolution, at other courts in Europe as well. Rosa Bonheur, a French 19th century painter, was best known for her animal paintings. Trained by her father (the only way girls received art training), she early showed great determination in the pursuit of her career and achieved early success as an animal painter. Later she was criticized for painting only animals, but it must be understood that girls were not permitted to draw from the life model.

In 1893 there was a building at the Chicago World Fair Columbian Exposition, designed by the woman architect Sophia Hayden, which was established and run by a board

"Children and a Dog," Sofonisba Anguissola, 16th century. (The Methuen collection)

"Self Portrait," Katharina van Hemessen, 1548. (Kunstmuseum, Basel)

"A Boy and a Girl with a Cat." Judith Leyster, 1609-1660. (The National Gallery, London)

"Charles Alexandre de Calonne, Comte d'
Hannonville, Baron d'Ornes," Elizabeth Vigée-
Lebrun, 18th century. (Copyright reserved)

"Portrait of Marie Antoinette," Elizabeth Vigée-Lebrun, 18th century. (Museum of History, Versailles)

"Self Portrait," Rosa Bonheur, 1822-1899. (Galleria degli Uffizi—Firenze)

of women managers. Emily Sartain of Philadelphia was chairwoman of the board from Pennsylvania. She was also one of the founders and first dean of Moore College of Art, the oldest art school for women in the country. The building contained artwork by women from around the world, including a large mural by Mary Cassatt, and Mrs. (Mary Fairchild) Macmonnies, whose full name was not mentioned. William Walton's comment in *World's Columbian Exposition, Art and Architecture*, concerning the mural was typical of the descriptions concerning women's work. He referred to Cassatt's mural as "overly sentimental," and the following statement appeared in the Exposition's program:

> Both [Cassatt and Macmonnies] placed their figures in long pleasant landscapes, though by so doing Mary Cassatt seems rather to have missed the point of her symbolism, as the occupation in which she has represented her "modern woman" — gathering fruit — is scarcely that which best corresponds to the high claims put forth for their share in modern civilization. Mrs. Macmonnies' primitive women were more appropriate in their household and domestic labors.

The female experience in visual perception can best be described by comparing a painting of a mother and child by Renoir to that of a work with the same subject by Mary Cassatt. Renoir painted many women, and one might imagine that he was ideally in love with women as we gaze at his many works. The following is a letter written by Renoir to his friend, the poet Catulle Mendes:

> I consider that women are monsters who are authors, lawyers, and politicians, like George Sand, Madam Adam, and other bores who are nothing more than five-legged beasts. The woman who is an artist is merely ri-

diculous. Gracefulness is woman's domain and even her duty. I know very well that today things have become worse, but what can we do?

This statement by Renoir hardly reflects the idea of respect and equality, and certainly not "love" for women. What do Renoir's paintings of women reflect about women? If we examine the three versions and numerous drawings of Renoir's wife, Aline, nursing their son Pierre, we can make an interesting observation. In each painting, Renoir focuses on his wife's exposed breast and the little boy's naked lower half. Aline gazes at the painter. She is not depicted as emotionally involved with little Pierre; Renoir paints his wife as a passive, decorative fruitcake, gazing soulfully at the artist.

Cassatt's mother and child, on the other hand, are depicted as actively involved with each other. In paintings and drawings by Cassatt having a mother-and-child theme, the mothers are caring for, nursing, engaged with, and generally portrayed as emotionally involved with their children.

Another example of painting from the "female experience" can be observed in the paintings by the French painter Berthe Morisot. In her work we observe women as self-contained beings actively involved in "doing things" rather than depicted as passive subjects splayed out frontally for male appreciation, as is Manet's "Olympia."

Women as well as men can find culturally relevant information in all aspects of Western culture, but the belittlement of women's contributions in the arts can no longer be tolerated. It isn't true that there have been no great women artists. We must no longer accept the "male-oriented" vision and perception with "universal" vision and perception, we are forced to see the world from a single perspective—as men see it. As long as the male artist's perception is taught to be the universal vision, no women's work which challenges those perceptions can be rightfully valued and honored.

The female experience becomes the "feminist" experi-

ence as we search through old periodicals and library basements, "excavating" tiny fragments of information concerning women's contributions. We have a great amount of "ex-
cavation" ahead of us. Women's historical contributions are
buried in books on shelves throughout libraries of the world.
The time has come to blow away the dust and cobwebs from
them as well as from our minds.

Female Iconography
at Stonehenge

I drove toward the Salisbury Plain in England with Lee Shaun, my daughter, anxiously anticipating our first visit to Stonehenge. It suddenly appeared unexpectedly on the horizon like a small cluster of rocks that had been clumped or carelessly dumped on the gently rolling expanse of green plain. This first visual confrontation surprised me, for I had studied Stonehenge in my college days and had seen documentaries about it on television, but this sight before me did not match the image I had developed. Soon, however, Lee Shaun and I would discover that the mystical drawing power that attracts thousands of tourists does not originate from mere physical size alone. Little did we realize that we were about to experience emotions that would remain with us for a long time, emotions that would later change and affect the direction of my work as an artist.

We parked our car nearby losing sight of Stonehenge for a moment as we were forced to enter the modern parking facility for tourists. We walked down to a concrete underpass where a man collected our admission fee which entitled us to walk through a modern structure beneath the highway and up a ramp to the grounds where the stones stood. Our initial enthusiasm was somewhat dampened by all the trappings of the twentieth-century entrance, but disappointment soon vanished as we stood transfixed when confronted with Stonehenge, feeling a quiet and somewhat foreboding atmosphere about us. Lee Shaun, who is usually excitable, became quiet, and we found ourselves talking in ridiculous whispers as we moved towards the stones which now loomed up, compelling us to draw nearer and to touch them. The wind roared across the plain and created drafts through the dolmens, stinging our faces and pushing around and against our backs as we moved between the huge pillars. The sensation that I was experiencing at that moment could only be referred to as a "gut reaction" to the place. Here was a primitive place filled with visual images of phallic and organic forms. Lee Shaun whispered, "It's scary, Mom!" At this point I was reminded of Jung's theory of the great collective unconscious. We certainly were both experiencing something that did not exist totally in our rational minds. There was no logic to what we were feeling and as Gerald S. Hawkins, author of Stonehenge Decoded, stated, "Stonehenge is wordless and correctly belongs to prehistory times," which perhaps best explains our emotions.

My curiosity aroused, we continued to walk outside the roped-off perimeter. As I stood looking at the various forms and contours against the gray English sky, Lee Shaun wandered off among the inner circle of stones. I walked alone circling one of the larger dolmens, and gently rubbing my hand over its smooth surface, experienced a mild sexual fantasy— conjured forth, I guess, by its texture and huge vertical erection. I felt its strength, and with my hand resting on it, felt a coldness creeping into and up my arm, while my eyes scanned the circle of large stones surrounding me on all sides. Suddenly I realized, as an artist, that I had seen these shapes and felt similar strength emanating from the paintings and

Stonehenge. (Photograph by Robert W. Ott)

drawings created by artists working from the female experience, organic, or yin, qualities of nature. Here was the very movement, color, power, and form found in Georgia O'Keeffe's work. These forms were familiar to me for I had seen them in work that filled galleries from New York to California. The dolmens with their ragged inner edges, all at various degrees of opening, not unsimilar to vaginas, were the very organic forms I had used in my own work as an artist. Some of the stones' ragged edges were close together so only a sliver of sunlight penetrated through them, while others were further apart allowing the light to pass through, expelling it and stretching wide. I truly believed at that moment I had come face to face with the visual source, the forms that created the inspiration for some of the most exciting art created by women, and sometimes men, buried in our collective unconscious centuries ago. Stonehenge was a superb déjà vu; filled with visual and emotional inspiration rising majestically from the moist earth, silhouetted against the changing sky of the English plain. Because I am an artist and my training is in the visual and intuitive processes, I experienced strong visual messages as well as intuitive feelings about Stonehenge. In Beyond Stonehenge, Gerald Hawkins states a similar idea: "My training is in physical science—quantitative, numerical—and naturally I tend to look for these aspects in prehistoric art. Prehistoric art should be looked at through all types of eyes, because by a composite integration we may approach something toward the original meaning." Henry Beston, in The Outermost House: "I had shared the elemental world." In each case, we were experiencing emotions very difficult to put into words. Later, I would find this frustration would lead me to expressing myself through a completely new series of drawings based on visual experiences at Stonehenge, experiences that I could not possibly illustrate with words alone.

My thoughts were interrupted by the voice of a lecturer who was addressing what appeared to be a group of English university students. Strangely, his voice rasped against my

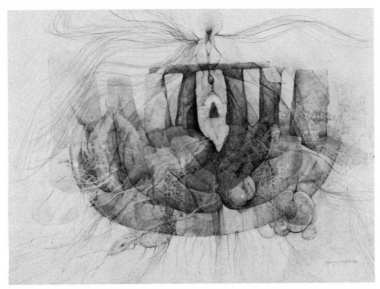

"Stonehenge #1," series, Joelynn Snyder-Ott, graphite drawing.

Stonehenge. (Photograph by Robert W. Ott)

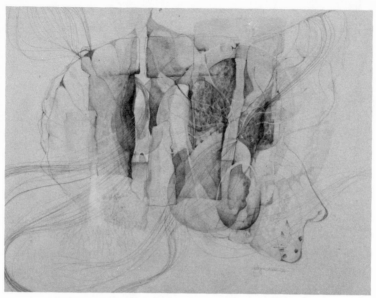

"Stonehenge #2," series, Joelynn Snyder-Ott, graphite drawing

ears and nerves like fingernails on a chalkboard. His upper-class voice, so coldly unemotional, sounded strange in such an emotion-laden atmosphere. He didn't fit in here, but I was not quite sure why. Eventually I realized that all his theories and "words, words, words," could not possibly carry the emotion in defining this place where words were meaningless in the presence of these mighty dolmens in the hot piercing sun, the damp wind, and the quiet foreboding atmosphere that surrounded us. The students among the group seemed self-conscious and oddly disoriented as they climbed over and around the large stones lying on the ground, slipping and laughing as they jockeyed for a favorable listening position. Remembering my own college art history classes, I listened as the lecturer continued with his "logical" explanations concerning the origins of Stonehenge. He then began talking about the many different theories including the idea of Stonehenge as a fertility worship place. I studied the women students' faces as he, rather bemusedly, explained this, all of course, from his male-oriented, Western patriarchal-religion background and perspective.

If indeed, Stonehenge was used as a fertility worship place, that use predates Christianity and the emergence of the patriarchal religions; it probably would have been created for a matriarchal religion, and therefore Stonehenge should be interpreted from a feminist or female-oriented viewpoint. Unfortunately, however, our Western religious background does not encourage the image of God as anything other than male. Male scholars have interpreted Stonehenge within a male-oriented structure of thinking. It's interesting to note that some earlier versions of the creation myth versions give importance to the woman, which in the *Book of Genesis* is accorded to the man, Adam. Woman's importance as childbearer was important in ancient religions, and descent of ancient family lineage was not through the father, but was matrilineal, through the mother.

Stonehenge. (Photograph by Robert W. Ott)

As the sun filtered through the openings between the stone posts, I was reminded of Bronislaw Malinowski's *Sexual Life of Savages in North-Western Melanesia*. He had written of the Trobriand Islanders that their creation beliefs were exclusively associated with women. They believed woman had created the sun, but kept a little of the fire for cooking, hiding the fire in her vagina when she wasn't in need of it. According to the myth, man discovered her hiding place and stole it.

As the wind continued to blow across the plain and through the dolmens, I was reminded of the story of Eurynome, a goddess of the Pelasgians of ancient Greece. Eurynome was impregnated by the wind in the shape of a serpent, and she later laid the world as an egg. Here, on this vast expanse of isolated plain, the English gales had blown for centuries, and with each gust their power was thrust between the awaiting dolmens. Suddenly the mythological story became a living experience. As the wind pushed against my body, every fiber of my being was experiencing the vibrations emanating from these rocks. My mind was racing, and I was struck again with the idea that this was an ancient woman's place. The quiet and enduring strength filled me with serenity, and the images of the stones produced a wealth of female iconography.

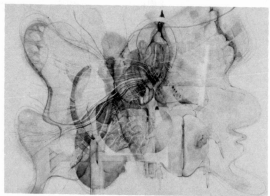

"Stonehenge #3," series, Joelynn Snyder-Ott, graphite drawing.

Many artists have experienced the subtle forces while at Stonehenge, receiving inspiration from their mighty organic forms. Henry Moore, the English sculptor, was so inspired by Stonehenge that he issued an entire series of graphic prints entitled "Stonehenge." The nineteenth century English writer, Thomas Hardy, was moved to write of it in *Tess of the d'Urbervilles, a Pure Woman.* He referred to Stonehenge as a "heathen temple" for sacrifice of humans. As a man, writing from a male perspective, he symbolically used Stonehenge as the setting where the men of the village found Tess sleeping on the "sacrifice stone." They carried her off to be executed, thus creating a symbolic sacrifice by her capture, on the very stone that may have been used by ancient matriarchs for other sacrifices.

"Stonehenge #4," series, Joelynn Snyder-Ott, graphite drawing.

It's easy to imagine Stonehenge in a feminist context, that is, seeing and perceiving it from a female-oriented perspective. The sun caresses and warms the stones, filtering through the openings between the dolmens, casting shadows on the round rocks inside the circle. The rocks on the ground inside the large circle are beautifully shaped—around their base, round stone forms appear like Earth Mother's embryonic sacs or the "world egg."

As I circled the outer area of Stonehenge where the Aubrey holes are located, named after the man who discovered them, I counted off each one. There are fifty-six outer holes. Perhaps they were used, as has been suggested, as some sort of a calendar. Since women existed before calendars and since our monthly cycles are usually a regular twenty-eight days, the fifty-six holes represented, possibly, two cycles. I was beginning to feel exhausted as I spotted Lee Shaun coming around a large stone.

She joined me, and we rested together, pressing our bodies against the ancient rocks. As we stood there, my daughter ran her hand down over the rock's surface. Suddenly she said, "Look! There's a sword design carved into this one." She pushed her finger into a tiny double-axe design, a design that I had seen used by the American Eskimo and called the *elu*. This double-axe is a symbol that has appeared in artwork from all corners of the globe, and in ancient times was always associated with the goddess. I took her hand and we walked away as quietly as we had come, leaving behind the lecturer, who was still talking, and the many tourists. Stonehenge had released our imaginations and had given us something that neither of us would soon forget. The spell was broken when we reached the underpass to our car. Returning to the twentieth century at the other end of the tunnel was swift and painless. Arriving tourists, talking loudly passed us, some stared curiously, for on our faces were etched the most ridiculous smiles of conspiratorial delight. Stonehenge belonged to us!

A View from England

As a self-confessed "uppity" feminist artist from the United States, I found living in England for a year rather similar to what I would imagine it is like to be suspended in a cool green bottle, gently rocking back and forth, fermenting like a vintage wine. The feminist struggle in England seems to be much more of a class struggle than a problem which is unique to women. Consequently, that year became one of introspection, with my mind lying fallow like a farmer's field, absorbing all the nutrients of a new environment. The idea of taking on and surmounting a whole class structure in order to reach the woman's problem seemed overwhelming, and one which certainly would take longer than one year of residency to tackle.

At London University, for instance, where I conducted a seminar on women and art, the students were interested in feminist art, but more from an anthropological than from a political viewpoint. One reason for this is the class structure. In England, women of the "professional class" have always been better tolerated as "equals" by men than, for example, the working-class woman. The majority of students in English universities are from this professional class, and unlike colleges and universities in the U.S. where the majority of students are from the middle- and even working-class homes, these students, as well as faculty, are considered "professional" or "upper class." The professional class in England is the governing class. Within this class structure have come all the women artists, writers and historians. Consequently, to take a feminist viewpoint at such an institution seems absurd. The professional woman, unlike the working-class woman, has no need to juggle career and family—her lifstyle has always been maintained by other women, namely those of the working class. An example of how this works can be seen in the television series "Upstairs-Downstairs." Although this series represents England during the nineteenth century, much of the social structure presented in this program is still in evidence today.

The feminist struggle in England will never be solved within the walls of the university. Feminism in England can be beneficial to the working-class woman, for it is within her class structure that the most blatant stereotypes of "woman's place" exists.

Since the nineteenth century, art education for women has been accepted as a "refined knowledge of the arts," and unfortunately this idea has persisted well into the twentieth century. During the seminar I conducted, it was related by one of the faculty members of the university that during the thirties at a London art school, an administrator told one of his assistants that every year he took the equivalent of one hundred students, and out of these students thirty were male, and seventy were female. The thirty men should be gifted, this administrator explained, and the women students should be good-looking and from excellent homes. Further, "We do not expect these women to become artists, but we expect them to learn some art, to understand some art, and then to marry rich industrialists, and buy pictures painted by their colleagues" (the male students). He made it quite clear that this would become a policy in order to create an art clientele or market. The faculty member relating this horror story continued that he actually knew people who had graduated from this art school in the 1930s, and who are still biased toward paintings because of this deliberate form of art patronage among the upper classes. This, of course, no longer exists at this school, but one wonders how many excellent women artists were lost to this system, a system that most probably was a universal phenomenon during the years of the "feminine mystique."

For years, as a student at Moore College of Art in Philadelphia, the oldest art school for women in the U.S., I was constantly reminded by male art student friends at other schools that because Moore was exclusively a "girls" school, we must then be "provincial" and also a "finishing school," rather than a "serious" art college. One can become very sympathetic with the amount of work the present administration, board members, and faculty at Moore must have endured to finally change this misconception, for originally, Moore College was begun as a feminist art school to train young women from working-class homes so they might obtain jobs in industry. Of course, there have been many outstanding women graduates of this institution. Alice Neel, one of the most important portrait painters of the twentieth century, is one example among many.

I've returned now to the United States, returning as a salmon fighting my way against the rushing current of America's special type of chauvinism, screaming speed, plastic gardens, and frozen dinners. America, with all its growing pains as a country, is the source of adrenalin, the instinctual impetus for my work as an artist and my life. The year of "fallowness" and "fermentation" was nourishment to my soul, a time to step off the treadmill and view my life and goals from an altered perspective. As an artist, it's beneficial, to a political activist, a rest to recharge before rejoining the struggle. There will remain with me forever, I think, a bit of England and her serenity, her images of Constable-like parks, the changing sky captured eternally by Turner, the meandering Thames unchanged since Sisley painted it, and the English people themselves, with their disdainful Reynolds smiles and delicate peach-tissue skin as painted and recorded so well by Angelica Kauffman in the eighteenth century.

To this experience I owe a new found serenity. My drawings have found a place in my new awareness. Reflecting on the drawing series I completed while in England I realized that as each form evolved and metamorphosed, images were appearing not totally from my conscious awareness. I cannot explain this by rules of ordinary sensory perception, the ways in which we come to know the external world, but rather it seems to belong to an intuitive phenomenon connected directly to the inner experience without an overemphasis or intervention of rational thought or influence. I experienced this same deep emotion when confronted with the organic and sensual megalithic stones and forms that surrounded me at Stonehenge—seeing in their form, color, and texture, ancient primordial images that had inspired artists throughout the centuries. In the drawing series entitled "Joie de Vivre—Birth/Rebirth," these images have become a personal joy of life, as well as a celebration of woman and the female found in the organic imagery of nature.

The year in England became then, in spite of the many class-structure frustrations, a memorable one. The memories, suspended now in that gently rocking cool green bottle, should hopefully make my future years vintage ones. For England, unlike the U.S., is a country basically "yin" oriented, more quietly sensitive and non-aggressive. For one year I lived in an environment free of the macho concept of aggressive competition. This concept of living does not create a world power or an efficient economy, but it does create, I found, happier human beings.

Women in Art

A few years ago, as a visiting lecturer in the art department at a large American university, I was asked to present a lecture on women and art which would be open to the general public as well as the students. I became aware that to talk about women in art I would first have to describe the conditions of women in general and how these conditions influenced the art which they produced. I had been reading every book concerning our history that I could lay my hands on— our political struggles as women, biographies, and articles written on developments within the women's liberation movement. I was, I thought, in a fairly aware state of consciousness concerning myself as a woman, and considered myself a feminist, and was toying with the idea of calling myself a "feminist artist." I felt angry enough about women's social conditioning that images of my anger were appearing in my work.

I had been invited to have a one-woman exhibit at the university which probably led to the later invitation for the open lecture. The exhibition caused an uproar, and I found it curious that this particular exhibit, with women as its major theme, should create a response more negative than the exhibit I had had previously where I had spilled my guts over the Vietnam tragedy. (The anti-war exhibit had received favorable press reviews in spite of the unpopularity of the exhibit's theme in a conservative area. One small exception was the reviewer who had suggested that any future exhibit like it would cause the "establishment" to deport me.) The invitations to the new exhibit stated that the exhibition was dedicated to the women's liberation movement, and all those strong and courageous sisters throughout our history whom I admired were listed on the cover of the invitation: Sojourner Truth, Mary Cady Stanton, Mary Wollstonecraft, women artists including Barbara Hepworth and Louise Nevelson (my mother), and two groups of organized political women: the National Organization for Women and the Women's Equity Action League. The latter inclusion probably caused the most distress, as WEAL was in the process of suing various universities for sex discrimination. Mention of their name was probably responsible for the summons for me to appear in an administrator's office of the university, where I was patronizingly advised that I should be spanked for my crazy women's lib ideas, "You're really not one of *those*?" I was also advised that I should not publicize my affiliation with the women's movement and my affiliation with the university at the same time. This was in 1972, before it was terribly radical-chic to be affiliated with the women's movement. At this point, the university was not amused by my political sympathy. This administrator was quite nasty, although he handled it in a patronizing manner. It was a friendly male sexist reprimand; he, acting as so many men (who love women and want them in their places), as the Edwardian father, chastising a child rather than an administrator confronting a professional employee. I was scared, for like most women I lacked the self-confidence, at the time, in my work and ideas. In the fashion of blacks, I "Yes, sir"-ed him, and slunk quietly out of his office. Nevertheless, the exhibit remained hanging, but I was advised to remove the "women's lib" brochure.

The "offending brochure" announcing the author's exhibition dedicated to women's liberation.

29

The response to the exhibit was fantastic, with some visitors filling entire pages of the exhibit register with comments—from women as well as men—and most were joyous, some vehement. The exhibit was my catharsis. In it I had rid myself of the poison of discontent that surely would have suffocated me and destroyed me as an artist. I was to experience a new surge of strength accompanied by an inner serenity.

Feeling at peace with myself—for a gigantic weight had been lifted from my senses—I turned from the objective to the subjective in my work. At last I was able to confront myself emotionally as a woman. Perhaps this increased state of awareness was partly a maturing process as a woman, but I began to explore within, working from my own experience as a woman, working as it were, from the experience of being female. I projected awe for my female body and likened what I found to the forms found in nature. I studied the designs and workings of flowers and even weeds. I was amazed at the similarity of my own body to the inner designs of flowers, the pink-lipped conch shells, and the overlapping and mysteriously unfolding petals and insides of vegetables and other organic plants. I slit open fruit and studied the interior—the seeds carefully concealed in an organic pouch of marvelous textures and linear configurations. The delicate coloring and fuzzy covered contours of peaches became an endless delight of female fantasy and iconography. Male artists have used the fruit metaphor, and one is reminded of Gauguin native girls holding the ripe mangoes on a tray under their naked breasts while gazing at the viewer with invitation painted in their eyes. Amusingly, I visualized the possibility of bananas. I became fascinated with mushrooms—those male-like organic forms that had appeared in so many women's drawings, paintings and sculpture. But this new source of inspiration was not the body of woman as an erotic object. I was not drawing female forms as male artists had done, as objects. I was seeing our beauty and strength, a strength that transcends a superficial erotic state-

"Joie de Vivre" series, Joelynn Snyder-Ott,
graphite drawing.

ment. I was working from a female experience and discovering myself as a woman, and nature as female, as the source, the subject, the strength.

This female phenomenon became a joy as I recognized female organic forms in Georgia O'Keeffe's work as well as Barbara Hepworth's sculpture. While in England, I came across John Berger's *Ways of Seeing*, based on a BBC television series. He devotes a chapter to the male artist's interpretation of woman as an object: "But the essential way of seeing women, the essential use to which their images are put, has not changed. Women are depicted in a quite different way from men—not because the feminine is different from the masculine—but because the "ideal" spectator is always assumed to be male and the image of the woman is designed to flatter him." Personally, I'm not interested in painting or drawing the male nude or doing a concentrated study of the male genitalia in the way male artists have painted women. I do feel, however, that women art students should be given the opportunity of painting and drawing the nude male model in life drawing classes, and that the male model should be posed, if the female student so wishes, in a position that is erotic for her to paint from the viewpoint of a woman.

For years women have seen slick magazines featuring erotic poses of women for men's perusal and enjoyment. Now we have slick magazines featuring men in sensual poses for women's perusal and enjoyment. Unfortunately, becoming "like the men" does not solve the problem. The slick magazine *Playgirl* is doing exactly the same thing to the male that the male-oriented magazines have done to the female, namely, a human being becomes an object rather than a human. When this happens, the person loses any identity and becomes merely an object, an object that is used to fulfill social, political or sexual stereotypes. Visual stereotypes of this order can be seen every day, such as the recent photograph of a politically active and powerful woman, pictured at the kitchen sink. Another example, of course, is children's books showing little girls always "helping" mother, playing house, while little boys are *doing* things: fixing, discovering, or experimenting.

As women then, stereotyping the images of men is not the answer, although one must admit that is great fun. Personally, I would like to see paintings and photographs of men, created by women, that capture a human sensitivity in their characters which for too long men have suppressed for fear they will be considered weak or emasculated.

My work, then, began to reflect an increased awareness, and I continued my writing, researching women's contributions in the arts, and consciousness-raising sessions with male and female students.

Researching women artists is a difficult, but rewarding task, and one begins to feel like an archaeologist, crying out in delight on finding a small reference to a woman artist buried or wedged in between long articles and color reproductions of a male artist's work. As Simone de Beauvoir states in *Force of Circumstance*, upon finding information, one must then try to pierce through the mythological, prejudicial and sexist documentation in which most women artists have been recorded, destroying the myth of femininity which usually veils women's accomplishments.

One such example of this prejudicial attitude can be found in the work of an outstanding woman portrait painter of the eighteenth century. For the past year I have been researching the life of Angelica Kauffman, one of the founders of the Royal Academy of Art in London. Previously, the only references to her in art history books have been to her as a "decorative painter" (elegant, charming and talented were a few more adjectives), and that was about all. In researching her life, I found that she was probably as popular as Sir Joshua Reynolds during her lifetime, and that she was certainly a rival to Gainsborough as well as other male portrait painters active in England during the period. Her decorative work for Robert Adam was only a very minor interest in her life. However, as a decorative painter, she is fulfilling society's role of a woman in the arts. Women have always been

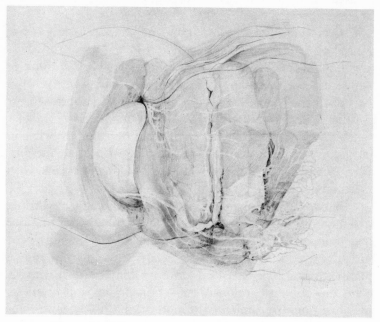

"Joie de Vivre" series, Joelynn˙ Snyder-Ott, graphite drawing.

tolerated and acclaimed as long as they stayed within the boundaries of fields allotted to them as women.

Researching the lives of other women artists led to further understanding of myself as an artist, and served as an impetus to encourage women students. Women artists, confronted with the problems of women living in a sexist society, represent excellent role-models for women students. I began to look at other women with new eyes as well, and found one surprise after another. It is both strange and stimulating, as Simone de Beauvoir states in *Force of Circumstance*, to discover after many years an aspect of the world that had been staring you in the face all the time, but somehow you never noticed. I decided to examine some figurative paintings by male artists that until this time I had always enjoyed, but had never considered because of the sex of the artist, and I was also interested in looking at women's work as a group.

I read Virginia Woolf's *A Room of One's Own,* and agreed with her idea that there exist both male and female value systems in literature, with the male value system prevailing. I agreed with de Beauvoir that woman is viewed as the object and never the subject, but I had never considered that this value system might exist in the visual arts. Thinking within this context then, I hurried to the art history library to obtain slides of women artists' work as well as examples of male artists' work, for I wanted to compare them to see if there actually was a difference in "vision."

My enthusiasm was immediately undermined when I realized that our art history library afforded very few examples of women's work. Slides that did exist were poor examples. One slide pictured artist Helen Frankenthaler sitting on the floor in front of her painting, her skirt swirled around her body. Obviously the photographer was working within a male context, he chose to concentrate on the woman Frankenthaler, rather than her work—the huge stained abstract painting in the background. There were a few examples of Kathe Kollwitz' work, but they were not her stronger pieces. I was unable to obtain any of her strong and dynamic self-portraits. I made a mental note to grumble to the faculty and left a cryptic message with the art history librarian to pass the word on to the head of the art history department. The lack of representation of women's work was appalling and deplorable. It had little effect at that time, but eventually we did get a course on women and art launched. In the meantime, I managed to collect about fifteen examples from the library, and borrowed the rest from women artist friends.

Viewing examples of women's work, I realized that it isn't very often one sees women's work as a group. Unlike the paintings of women made by male artists, these examples were honest and direct. They did not represent masculine fantasies about women. As Judy Chicago stated in *Through the Flower,* the images of women painted by women were not presented as fleshy, secular nudes, or veiled in religious or mythological significance. They contained no idealizations of purity and maternity, maidens and madonnas, and male sexual fantasy stereotypes. I suddenly realized that what I had been taught, and indeed, what I believed, never included this idea. Most of the paintings that I was now viewing by Renoir, Modigliani, Manet, Goya and de Kooning, to name a few, were all examples of a male sexual fantasy. Where then, were the paintings by women artists of men in the same kind of sexual fantasy poses? There were none. Only women smiled out at me with invitation painted into their eyes and mouths by male artists. What I was viewing was how one half of the population viewed the other half. Where was the male counterpart of "Olympia" as painted by Manet? Why weren't women allowed to paint men as men had always painted women? Why did life drawing classes in art schools and universities use mostly female models for their art students, when many times there were more women students enrolled in the life classes than male students?

Recently I returned with my daughter, Lee Shaun, to the National Portrait Gallery in London, to point out to her the self-portrait of Angelica Kauffman. Earlier in the year, I was pleased to see Kauffman's portrait hung in the room in a prominent place under the general heading, "Grand Manner," for indeed she was one of the leaders of this school of painting. Also represented there were works by Reynolds, Fuseli, Hone, Hogarth, and Gainsborough. Here was one of the founders of the Royal Academy, who was considered "mother of all the eighteenth century arts."*

She was as highly respected and honored as Reynolds, and would one day leave England with 14,000 pounds sterling in portrait commissions, twice as much as her artist hus-

---

Angelica Kauffman, Her Life and Work by Lady Victoria Manners, and Dr. G.C. Williamson. John Lane, the Bodley Head Ltd. 1924 (from the eulogy at her funeral).

"The Fruit of the Womb," ("Joie de Vivre" series),
Joelynn Snyder-Ott, graphite drawing.

band, Antonio Zucchi. Her decoration and porcelain pieces
would serve as an influence for generations of decorative
work. Almost every European museum has some representation of her work, including the University of Pennsylvania.
She had succeeded in spite of many frustrations brought
about simply because she was a female. She managed to
study in the European galleries only after disguising herself
as a boy (as many women artists were forced to do, since
women were not permitted to study in the museums and galleries.) She was more popular than many of her contemporaries whose works were hanging with hers in the National
Gallery. And yet, in spite of her great achievements, she has
been poorly documented. Her biographers have been more
concerned with her charm and elegance rather than with her
work.

But now it was spring, we had returned to have another look. She was gone, and hanging in her place of honor was a recent acquisition by Reynolds. As I looked around at the many examples of Reynolds' work already hanging there, my conviction was reconfirmed. There was not one woman artist represented in this room, and yet in the nineteenth century, there were recorded the names of 3,000 women artists in Great Britain. They were, as Angelica Kauffman's work, most probably gathering damp rot in museum basements. It was difficult to explain to my daughter why they put away the only example of a woman's fine work in the room when they had so many poorer examples of male artists' work. I thought of all the school children who paraded by these paintings never having the opportunity to see paintings by women artists; perpetuating the myth that the great artist is always "male."

As women artists and art instructors have begun to realize, we can all find culturally relevant information in all aspects of Western culture, but we can no longer tolerate the belittlement of women's contributions in the arts. It just isn't true that there are no great women artists. The fault does not lie with us as women, but in trusting the documentation of our contributions to the male historian and *his*-tory! For as long as we continue to accept the male artist's vision as the only vision, regardless of women's perceptions, then no women's work which challenges those perceptions can be rightfully valued and honored for its own intrinsic value. We must destroy the myths that bring about findings such as the P. Goldberg study, "Are Women Prejudicial Against Women?" (*Transition,* April 1969).

In this study, conducted in the U.S. and published in 1969, it was found that even when women do achieve on a "par" with men it would not be perceived or accepted as such, and that a woman's work must be of a much higher quality than that of a man to be given the same recognition. He found, that although girls make consistently better grades than boys until late high school, their opinions of themselves

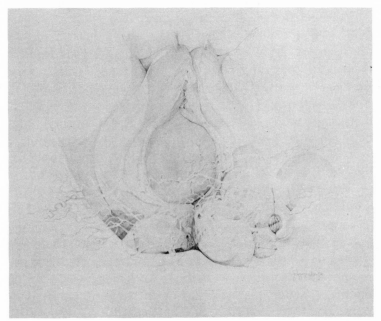

"Among the Roots, Golden Threads are Glistening," ("Joie de Vivre" series), Joelynn Snyder-Ott,
graphite drawing.

grows progressively worse with age and their opinion of
boys increasingly better. Boys, however, have an increasingly better opinion of themselves and worse opinion of girls.
These distortions become so gross, according to Goldberg,
that by the time girls reach college they have become prejudiced against women. He gave college women sets of book-
lets containing six identical professional articles in tradi-
tional male/female and neutral fields. The articles were identical, but the names of the authors were not. For example, an
article in one set would bear the name of "John T. McKay"
and in another set the same article would be authored by
"Joan T. McKay." Each booklet contained three articles by
"women" and three by "men." Questions at the end of each
article asked the students to rate the article's value, persua-

siveness and profundity, and the authors on writing style and competence. The "male" authors fared better in every field, while the identical articles with the women's names received more negative response. Goldberg concluded that women are prejudiced against female professionals and, regardless of the actual accomplishments of these professionals, will firmly refuse to recognize them as the equals of their male colleagues. One realizes the horror of this study's implications when studying the paintings of, for example, a "Violet" Van Gogh, rather than "Vincent," or a "Pauline" Picasso.

Women as well as men can find help in feminism, help, that is, which will bring about a raised consciousness. This new awareness for each of us as individuals will help to destroy so many of the devastating stereotypes that have locked women into various roles and expectations. There is a warning, however, for those who decide to change the system. As an outspoken feminist one must be prepared for personal attacks. You will be attacked and your family will be verbally berated. Your husband or lover's sexual prowess will be discussed, as society assumes there must be something wrong with your personal relationship to make you so "nutty." An example of this was a review in the London *Times* of Erica Jong's *Fear of Flying*. The reviewer (a woman, Tina Brown) stated: "*Fear of Flying* is a book with liberated female erotic fantasies . . . a bestseller in America, but a flop in Great Britain. She continued: "Mrs. [sic] Jong's husband stuck his head around the door and ducked out again with the hunted air of a man who has just guessed—accurately—that the lady journalist staring beadily at him from the sofa was speculating feverishly about his impeccable genitalia." Obviously the reviewer was more concerned with what she considered was Jong's problem than with her writing. She was keenly interested in Jong's husband and his genitalia, never mind the book.

Another trick used by men who wish to intimidate

feminists is the old line, "What's wrong with you?" followed by the answer, "What you need is a good lay," or "Good sex will cure you of your crazy ideas." You must be prepared to have words hurled at you such as : "unsatisfied," "frigid," "nymphomaniac," "ugly castrating bitch," "neurotic," "lesbian," and, the old standby, "penis envy." At social gatherings some men will enjoy the tradition of licentious talk (for your benefit) which provides them with a whole arsenal calculated to reduce you to your function as a sexual object. Some women too, will surprise you by joining in with them. We, as feminists, must be patient with these women, for they are the ones that have internalized the male-value social structure, and to pull the rug out from under their feet without substituting something constructive is bound to cause panic in their minds.

Referring to women who are searching for truth as "women-libbers"—a phrase coined by the male-dominated press—forces people to immediately classify all outspoken women, categorizing them and shoving them into a compartment so their ideas and individual philosophies don't have to be confronted and dealt with. Women are all individuals, some at different levels of consciousness. Women's liberation is a political movement, while the term "women's lib" is a put-down sounding more like a disease associated with some sort of female disorder.

We must destroy the myths that perpetuate women's inferiority and weakness, silliness, giddiness. These attitudes create the reviews of women's work, for instance, that miss entirely the point of the artwork, but concentrate on the woman's elegance, her marital state, her lover's virility, or simply concentrates on her as a physical object.

Feminism, then, is not becoming like men, or refuting what men say, but as women we must express ourselves truthfully, finding what we are about. We must destroy the stereotypes about us, not the men. As artists we will then be able to recognize the yin and yang that exists within us all.

A Woman's Place

Women's art, women's exhibitions, women's galleries, and discussions of a "female imagery" in the arts are thought to phenomena of the '70s. Women's contributions in the arts generally have been so poorly recorded, and seldom mentioned, that the entire feminist art movement seems new. However, it is not a new phenomenon at all. Our sisters of the previous century fought for equality in the arts just as militantly as are women artists today.

In 1892, for example, at the World's Columbian Exposition held in Chicago, women artists from around the world came together to demand representation at the Fair. The visibility of women working at the Centennial exhibition in Philadelphia in 1876 had proven to the public that they were thoroughly capable of making major contributions. When the matter was brought before the World's Fair Committee of the U.S. Congress, the representative from Illinois, a Mr. Springer, willingly inserted a clause authorizing the creation of a board of women managers with each member representing a state or territory, and championed it before the House where it met with no serious opposition.

The idea for a "Woman's Building" was conceived by the chairwoman of the board, Bertha Honore Palmer of Chicago. The board then issued the following statement concerning the idea for such a building: "The World's Fair Columbian Exposition should afford women an unprecedented opportunity to present to the world a justification of women's claim to be placed in complete equality with men. Women will have the opportunity to come from all quarters of the globe for the purpose of gathering evidence and demanding a hearing by the court of assembled nations, and further, the building will direct attention to women's progress and development, and her increased usefulness in the arts, sciences, manufacturing, and industries of the world during the past four hundred years and present a complete picture of the condition of women in every country of the world, and more particularly of those women who are the breadwinners."

It was decided by the women managers that a design for the building should be decided upon from sketches submitted by women architects, and "none but those made by women should be considered." Thirteen designs were submitted, and the winner was Sophia Hayden, a twenty-two-year-old woman from Massachusetts. She was awarded $1,000 for her design (a sum that later would annoy many women, and rightly so, as being inadequate for the amount of work involved.) Second prize of $500 went to the architect Lois Howe of Boston, and Laura Hayes, an architect from Chicago received a $250 third prize.

As today among women artists, not all women were in total agreement with the idea of segregating women's art from men's art. Louise Blanchard Bethune, an architect from New York, was perhaps the most outspoken critic of the idea of a "Women's Building." Bethune had studied in an architect's office, and then opened shop in upstate New York where she designed some eighteen schools in western New York, as well as stores and apartment houses. She was highly respected and was the first professional woman architect in

The Woman's Building of the World's Columbian Exposition in Chicago, 1893. (*World's Columbian Exposition: Art and Architecture,* William Walton)

the United States. Her criticism is almost identical to the opposition voiced today by some opponents of women's art although in all fairness to Bethune, she was more opposed to the idea of competition than against other women architects and artists. Her comment: "Competition is evil. I think the competition for the "Woman's Building" is the most objectionable form of competition, since it was by women and for women, and since it [the contest] was not conducted on the principle of equal pay for equal service." Her point was well taken. She did not submit a design.

Sophia Hayden, the winner of the commission, was the first woman graduate of the architectural course at the Massachusetts Institute of Technology. She was born in 1871 in Santiago, Chile; her father was from New England and her mother was South American. In her final year at M.I.T., she presented her thesis which was a design for a museum of fine arts which, with its Renaissance style, foreshadowed the design for the "Woman's Building" and epitomized the classic academic training she had received.

Sophia watched her building materialize from drawing board sketch to finished reality. The building included a gallery of honor which would house the paintings of outstanding women artists from around the world including the works of Mary Cassatt and Cecilia Beaux, watercolors from Queen Victoria, oil paintings from Princess Christian of Great Britain, a map created by a woman who lived at the time of Dante. There would be ceramics, pottery, needlework, an exhibit of the "evolution of macramé from simple knots to fine lace," stained glass, weavings, and inventions by women. Sophia's building would be the first to rise on the site of the Exposition. Compared with other Exposition buildings that were designed by men, the "Woman's Building" was small. The sum appropriated for it, only $200,000, was small compared to the appropriations in the millions given to buildings designed by male architects. The "Woman's Building" became overcrowded when it was forced to exhibit additional work by women artists who were denied space elsewhere.

The building was a masterpiece of classical style. Sophia Hayden's name was carved into the cornerstone, and women artists acclaimed the building and its contents as an example for other women so that they too would cultivate their talents and ambitions. Mr. Richard Hunt, president of the American League of Architects, awarded a medal to Hayden for "delicacy of style, artistic taste, geniality, and elegance." The critic for the *American Architect Magazine* responded however in a tradition familiar to women artists in the 1970s: "The building is neither worse nor better than might have been expected. The roof garden that crowns the building is a "hen-coop" for petticoated hens, old and young. It seems a question not yet answered how successfully a woman with her physical limitations can enter and engage in a profession which is a very wearing one." Bertha Honore Palmer, chairwoman of the board, ignored the carping of the critics and issued the following statement concerning criticism: "Nothing is more significant concerning the 'Woman's Building' than

Interior of the Woman's Building of the World's Columbian Exposition in Chicago, 1893. (*World's Columbian Exposition: Art and Architecture*, William Walton)

none of the critics said it looked like a man's work. Twenty years ago to be called strong-minded was a reproach which brought the blood to the cheek of many a woman. Today there are a few of our sisters who prefer to be classed among strong-minded rather than among weak-minded women."

Rumors were circulated about Sophia Hayden's mental health, that as a result of overwork she had broken down. Despite reports of mental exhaustion, Sophia was present at the dedication of her building to hear Palmer's dedicatory remarks: "Even more important than the discovery of Columbus, which we are gathered together to celebrate, is the fact that the General Government has just discovered women."

The monumental statuary atop the "Woman's Building" was designed by Alice Rideout, a nineteen-year-old woman from San Francisco, California. The theme of her sculpture was presented in three groups: Woman's Virtues, Woman as the Genius of Civilization, and Woman's Place in History. The models she created for the final pieces were enlarged to "heroic size" by Enid Yandell of Louisville, Kentucky, who modeled the caryatids to support the roof garden.

The American Minister in London arranged for the chairwoman of the board, Ms. Palmer, a private audience with her Royal Highness, Princess Christian. The princess suggested formation of an English women's committee for the Exposition. However, not all countries cooperated. The Tunisian government sent a letter stating that a commission of women could not be formed in Tunisia, because local prejudice did not allow the women to take part in public affairs. Syria responded in the same manner along with India, and countries of the Orient. Her Majesty, the Queen of Siam, however, sent a delegation. The Queen instructed the women's delegation from her country to study what industrial and educational advantages are open to women in other countries.

And so, women artists, and women visitors from

around the globe arrived at the "Woman's Building." Entering the building, the rotunda was the most prominent feature. The walls were covered by two murals, one by Mary Cassatt, and the other by Mary Fairchild MacMonnies. MacMonnies chose "Primitive Woman" as her theme, and Cassatt chose "Modern Woman." A male critic writing about the two murals praised MacMonnies' interpretation as more typical of women because she portrayed her women in the more "suitable role of domesticity." He chided Cassatt for her depiction of woman as gathering fruit.

The Gallery of Honor was created to show the high rank that had been obtained in art, science, literature, and industry by exceptional women in all parts of the world during the four centuries of the Columbian era, and also the diversified achievements of women of their own day with the view of showing the great change in their relation to practical affairs and the marked increase in their usefulness. There was a library lined with books and displaying a bust of Harriet Beecher Stowe, along with a cabinet containing copies of her forty-two translations of *Uncle Tom's Cabin*. There were frames containing autographs of the most famous women of the world. Living women authors of the day sent complete sets of their work.

Painters represented in the Gallery of Honor were Mary Cassatt, Cecilia Beaux, Enrilda Loomis France, and Ida Waugh. History has recorded Mary Cassatt, but one is astonished at the lack of documentation in later art history texts concerning Cassatt's contemporaries.

For instance, Cecilia Beaux was born in Philadelphia in 1863. Her first teacher was a woman. The first of her works to bring her fame was a painting entitled "Last Days of Infancy" which was exhibited at the Pennsylvania Academy of Fine Arts in 1885, and won the prize for the best painting by a resident woman artist. She won the same prize in consecutive years to follow. She spent the winter of 1889 to 1890 in Paris studying in the life classes of the Academie Julien. After

"Women Gathering Fruit," Mary Cassatt, 1893.
Exhibited in the Woman's Building, World Columbian Exposition, 1893. (*World's Columbian Exposition: Art and Architecture*, William Walton)

a visit to Italy and England, she returned to Philadelphia. In 1893, she won the gold medal of the Philadelphia Art Club for a portrait. She won the Dodge Prize of the National Academy of Design. Beaux was the seventh woman to be awarded the honor of election to membership in the Society of American Artists.

In 1894 she was elected associate of the National Academy of Design, being the third woman to gain admission. She became a full member in 1902. Her paintings were recognized and hung in major exhibitions both in the United States and abroad. Critics referred to her work as "brilliant." Her earlier paintings have been compared to Whistler in composition and setting. One is at a loss to explain why Cecilia Beaux is not recognized in most contemporary art history texts.

Feminists today are sometimes accused of relating only to the middle- and upper-class women of our society. The women managers were aware of this problem also, and in the spring of 1892, Bertha Honore Palmer called a meeting to discuss what could be done for wage-earning and industrial women of the country who might desire to visit the Exposition, but couldn't afford to come because of the expense of food and lodging. Matilda B. Carse, of the board, presented a plan to erect a women's dormitory. The plan was accepted and the dormitory was erected in a pleasant portion of Hyde Park, near the fairgrounds. A line of "wagonettes" made regular trips to and from the grounds, affording lower-income women an opportunity to share in this great moment of women's history.

Recently I visited Chicago, and I walked to Jackson Park where the Exposition had taken place. As I stood on the grounds, watching Lake Michigan gently lick the shore on one side of the park, I though of Bertha Honore Palmer's words: ". . . an unprecedented opportunity . . . complete equality . . . women will be emancipated . . . ." I visualized the magnificent "Woman's Building," filled with our history.

As I watched the roaring jets that have replaced the "wagon-ettes," I thought, "Why didn't I know of all this before? Why did I have to gather this information piece by piece from many sources?" The event that happened in Jackson Park was part of our history. It is too important to be trusted to *his*-tory.

Art As Yin in a
Yang Society

For many artists and 'sage' art educators, the ideal in life is
achieved through the practice of the Tao's ancient Chinese
concept of Yin and Yang, a concept that reflects a perfect
balance between polarities: *yin* representing the feminine and
yang the masculine. When these two aspects are working together, a perfect balance is achieved and neither element becomes more important than the other. One example of this
can be found in classical Greek culture where the balance between the masculine and feminine traits was in perfect har-
mony, and can be seen symbolized by the goddess, Athena,
who first of all, was a goddess of war—but benevolent and
compassionate—she was also the guardian of cities and later
became known as the goddess of wisdom. Traditionally, in
Western society, (a society strong on patriarchal religious beliefs and customs), yang, or the masculine, is considered
more important than yin; consequently anything existing in
opposition to yang, is regarded as of secondary importance.
In simple terms: The masculine is more important than the
feminine.

   Intuitiveness, moodiness, sensitivity, and weakness are

considered yin qualities, while aggressiveness, stoicism, boldness, and strength are considered yang qualities. They are described as yin and yang simply because they are opposites. This concept is brilliantly illustrated in Richard Wilhelm's *Book of Changes*, translated from the *I Ching, Book of Changes*. In this book various living things project either yin or yang principles in their roles in time, space, and the evolution of their creation and being. When applied to humans, these qualities are human emotions, which we all experience, in various degrees of each, at one time or another. Somewhere in our development, however, the yin and yang principles have gotten mixed up with genital characteristics, and Western society has delegated all humans with wombs as being intuitive, moody, sensitive, and weak. On the other hand, those possessing a penis are expected to be bold, aggressive, stoic, and strong. This concept has such a hold on our psyches that any human possessing the male genitalia is discouraged from expressing yin qualities, and those with female genitalia are encouraged to exhibit only yin qualities. In our Western society then, the feminine qualities of our personalities are still desperately awaiting rediscovery. What was once viewed, in ancient cultures, as an integration and balance between the feminine and the masculine, has become for us a grossly distorted and very one-sided situation. Yang, or the masculine qualities are still encouraged and developed to the exclusion of yin qualities. A rather vulgar example of this can be cited by noting the descriptive adjectives concerning these qualities existing not too long ago in school children. Young girls who are bold and aggressive are now encouraged and gently referred to as "tomboys." Boys, on the other hand, who exhibit traits of sensitivity (and artistic endeavors usually fall into this category) are commonly discouraged or described as "sissies."

How does this principle of yin and yang affect the artist and art teacher? Let us consider a rather simplistic, but pertinent example concerning the relationship of yin and yang to art, the artist, and the teaching of art in our schools. The arts

Mother goddess figure from Hacilar, Anatolia,
circa 5700-5600, B.C. (Archaeological Museum,
Ankara)

in most school programs are viewed as a polarity to the sciences. The sciences are usually described as logical, scientific, controlled rather than metamorphic, and logical rather than intuitive. The arts on the other hand exhibit more yin qualities and can be described as intuitive, sensitive, organic, and humanistic. With these two disciplines as polarities, let us make an honest evaluation of how our Western society views their intrinsic value. Every art teacher in the United States knows without reading further which discipline is more valued. When there is a budget cut, which goes first, a science subject or the art program? Art programs that do exist in most of our schools exist (as all yin elements) as a service or complement to the more valued yang disciplines. Only a few administrators, teachers, and parents recognize the importance of a strong art program within the curriculum—viewing the arts as a balance of the yin qualities with the strongly established yang disciplines, seeing the arts as an integration of important factors needed to develop the total personalities of students, rather than the lopsided state of affairs we have now.

In an article I wrote for the *National Art Education Journal* in 1974, I stated that the masculine values prevailed in art, that our society was "male-dominated" and "male-oriented." Today, I see the problem as going beyond mere genital differences. The elements that I was grappling with were society's reinforcement of yang ideals and the subsequent neglect of the yin factors and values. For instance, the slogan "You've gotta have art," that the American National Art Education Association had repetitiously printed on everything from shirts to buttons, becomes empty without our understanding of why it is we don't have art. As an art teacher I *know* "You've gotta have art," but a more important question is how militant are we willing to become to see that slogan changed to a more relevant one of "ART-naturally" a slogan employed by the Canadian Art Education Association. In this respect, art educators can learn a great deal from the tactics employed by the feminists and minorities demanding equal rights. We must begin to face the real problem and find solutions, for at present society still believes firmly that art is a frill and art teachers and their subjects are expendable.

As a beginning we need to educate ourselves to the value and importance of yin qualities. One way to do this is to study the past. Unfortunately, the classics are no longer stressed in our school curricula. This is unfortunate since the classics and the study of ancient civilizations are important in becoming aware of the female element, or yin factors, and their subsequent contributions to our civilization. For example, Lucy Lippard presented the question in her article in *Art News*, "Women's Body Art: The Pains and Pleasures of Rebirth": "Why haven't contemporary artists dealt with the subject of birth imagery?" Perhaps not many contemporary artists have created from this yin-oriented subject, but certainly our ancient religions are filled with this iconography. The fertility theme in ancient religions was treated much differently than today, however.

In the Dumuzi-Inanna and Osiris-Isis relationships, women in many ways always predominated and their figures, carvings, paintings, and female iconography predominated throughout early civilization. Patriarchal religions repressed female sexuality, however, and later religions inspired art that depicted birth, for instance, as a spiritual rather than a physical phenomenon as it was originally portrayed by early artists. In ancient societies, however, birth was the power of woman, and this yin principle continued into Christian, Saxon and Norman times, acting as a kind of balance to the yang or male-dominated patriarchal religion.

Another example of the yin element in ancient civilization can be found in an eleventh century church at Whittlesford, Cambridgeshire, England. There, on a medieval church, there are certain stone carved figures which have no obvious connection with Christian iconography. These figures are not inconsiderable in size, as they measure from about six

Mother goddess figure from Catal Huyuk, Anatolia. Early 6th century, B.C. (Archaeological Museum, Ankara)

"Sheela-na-Gig." (Crown Copyright)

inches to two feet in height and were called "Sheelas." They take the form of a woman with a grotesquely enlarged vagina usually held open with one or both hands. The woman is flanked by a "supporter" having an animal's head and a naked man's body, the stiff penis and testicles being depicted at the ready. Such overt emphasis on sexuality was hardly to be tolerated by an established male and yang-dominated Christian clergy who, from the time of Christ himself through St. Paul, had played down earthly love, had made a fetish, in fact, of celibacy in men and virginity in women, and had turned the Earth Mother into the Blessed Virgin Mary of the Immaculate Conception. Even after Reformation, the newly organized Anglican Church and its later Puritan, Wesleyan and other nonconformist offshoots set themselves sternly against flesh and the Devil (*flesh* meaning sexuality, whether in or out of wedlock).* I mention these facts to help redefine the yin or feminine elements in our rich ancient past, a past that has been referred to as "pagan," but nevertheless offers a wealth of female, or yin, iconography.

Other yin, or female, iconography can be found at Stonehenge, in the cave of Psychro, the palace of Knossos, and among many of the Indians living today in the backwoods of Canada. This iconography takes the form of the double axe. It is one of the most famous and frequent symbols of all, and was a feminine symbol as well as being one of the emblems of the goddess. It may have begun its evolution as a practical tool, into a religious symbol as an instrument of sacrifice comparable to the cross. Its shape, the double triangle, was widely used as a sign for woman, and the shaft thrust through the central axis affords an effective piece of sexual imagery.

Double axes can be found in the phallic stalagmites in the cave of Psychro. At Stonehenge one is carved into one of the dolmens. Always and everywhere the double axe is associated with the goddess, never with any male divinity. In

---

*The Lost Gods of England, Brian Branston, Oxford University Press.

Double axe in pottery, from cave of Eileithyia,
post 1400. Source of butterfly imagery? (*Dawn of
the Gods*, Jacquetta Hawkes. Random House,
Inc., New York. Photograph by Dimitrios
Harissiadis.)

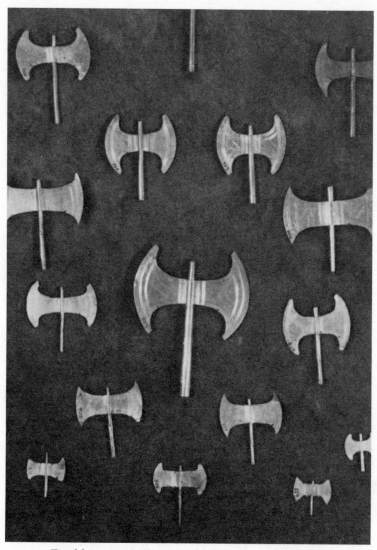

Double axes. (*Dawn of the Gods*, Jacquetta Hawkes. Random, Inc., New York. Photograph by Dimitrios Harissiadis.)

Crete, it came to have supreme significance as a symbol of the goddess. It was known there as the *labrys* from its Lydian name, and the palace of Knossos was known as the *Labyrinth* in the sense of the "House of the Double Axe." It was only later, when visiting Greeks saw the bewildering ruins of the ancient palace, that the name came to be applied to a maze. In the palace, as everywhere else, the double axe symbol was displayed as frequently and conspicuously as was the cross in Christian buildings. The double axe later evolved as the Celtic cross, and later, the Maltese cross. Its imagery and variations can be seen even today in much female iconography created by contemporary artists. One can trace this ancient symbol as the root iconography for many yin images; for example, the double axe began as the "labrys." Contemporary women artists using their own bodies as a source of imagery in their work are borrowing an ancient symbol used by the early Cretans. Even the female sexual anatomy is referred to as the "labial." When viewed historically, contemporary female iconography is no longer shocking.

Taking the image of the double axe as far as one can, the butterfly form used as part of a yin iconography is also a direct descendant, graphically, of the ancient double axe. Consequently, the butterfly has always maintained its feminine connotation, a relationship that has existed since ancient times. Double axes can be found in pottery such as those found in the Eileithyia cave, which dates 1400 B.C. At first glance these pottery forms look like, and are decorated very similarly to, the wings of butterflies.

It is time we acknowledge the continued, though repressed, existence of feminine symbolism, and the equal importance of both yin and yang elements in our lives, recognizing and reaffirming these elements in ourselves as well as seeing them in nature. An overemphasis of yang ideas and its dangers to all of us can be seen when we observe our society and what is happening to it. Aggressiveness, a yang quality, can be valuable when balanced by the yin quality of sensitiv-

"The Immaculate Conception," Bartolome Murillio, circa 1600. The strength and honesty found in the ancient female figures is missing in this later patriarchal religious portrayal. Woman, once portrayed as a strong, fertile earth-mother, has become in this painting a child-like woman. Birth here is portrayed as spiritual rather than physical. With this portrayal, woman loses control over her own body. (Museo del Prado, Madrid)

"Venus of Willendorf." Woman lost her portrayal as a sturdy earth-mother and began to be portrayed child-like and innocent as birth and sexuality became spiritual rather than physical and influenced by religion. (Naturhistorisches Museum, Wein)

ity. Without this balance there is war, murder, napalmed children, and raped and brutalized humans. Technology, a yang factor, becomes dangerously ruthless without the yin qualities that assure respect and a sensitivity for nature. Polluted water, fouled air and earth have come about by this inbalance, this overemphasis of yang.

Another example of imbalance is Hitler's Germany. The "Fatherland" with all the atrocities against humankind, carried out in a very systematic and logical manner, is probably one of the most frightening. Yang elements in such instances obviously far outweigh any yin elements; yin qualities were suppressed as a sign of weakness; only logic, exaggerated discipline, and aggressiveness were worth developing. It's interesting to note the kind of artwork produced by the Third Reich: two-dimensional social propaganda, lacking any yin qualities or emotion of any kind. Emotions elicited by viewing the artwork were yang emotions, emotions that roused the viewer to aggressively "join the forces."

It is only after we come to respect the female or yin qualities, giving these values an *equal* importance one with the other, that we will experience a oneness with each other that will be reflected in our art, and our attitudes to each other. As the sun and moon are considered polar forces, one being neither more important than the other but complementary, we too need to find our yin selves. It is this balance of forces within our personalities that we have neglected so grossly. The problem cannot be solved in a superficial debate between men and women. We must go much deeper to the source of the imbalance. The change must come first from within each of us as individuals; by changing our own consciousness, we will light one candle in a society which at present is darkly inimical to all qualities yin, and grossly negative to all programs relating to art. Until that time comes through education, the teaching of art and all qualities yin will continue to be inimical to our Western culture, and no amount of legislation, fine art programs, or bombardment of statistics will alter the situation. When Western society finally acknowledges the equal importance of yin qualities, only then will the artist, the art teacher, and the arts in the school and in society be valued in a symbiotic relationship of oneness.

Angelica Kauffman: Rival to Gainsborough

Angelica Kauffman was one of the most outstanding women painters of the eighteenth century. She was a founding member of the Royal Academy in London, and her work can be found (if searched out) in most major museum collections both in the United States as well as in England and Europe. She is of particular interest because she was a very famous painter during her lifetime, but her life and work have been poorly recorded, as has that of so many other women artists. Her contributions to Western art have been buried or wedged between page-long articles and huge color reproductions of her male contemporaries—even though many of them were not as outstanding as Kauffman.

Portrait painting in the eighteenth century was at its height in England. The style in which portraits were executed by the English artists was referred to as the "Grand Manner." This style, with Angelica Kauffman as its leading exponent, was eventually imitated and adopted by America's early portrait painters. Charles Wilson Peale of Philadelphia, a well-

69

"Portrait of Angelica Kauffman," Sir Joshua Reynolds. (Österreichisches Museum fur angewandte Kunst, Wein)

known American colonial portrait painter, was so impressed by Kauffman that he named his daughter Angelica Kauffman Peale. When the young Swiss woman, Angelica Kauffman, arrived in England from Rome with her patron and friend, Lady Wentworth, wife of the British ambassador, who had been living in Rome, she joined Sir Joshua Reynolds, Gainsborough, Ramsey, Zoffnay, and Copley. Her reputation had preceded her to London, for she had been painting portraits from her studio in Rome, painting the important patrons who were visiting there on the "Grand Tour." Sir Joshua Reynolds was the first to hear of her arrival in England. He was soon introduced to this new rival, but was so impressed

"Portrait of Sir Joshua Reynolds," Angelica Kauffman, 1741-1807. (The National Trust, Saltram)

with her style that he in turn introduced her to even more important patrons. Gainsborough, on the other hand, felt threatened by Angelica and remained somewhat at a distance from her and the social life of London. He never became friends with her, but remained aloof, painting most of his portraits from the city of Bath.

Angelica, on the other hand, was caught up in the social and intellectual life of London. Her first commission was for the Duchess of Brunswick. After successfully completing the portrait, she was inundated with patrons and work. She was introduced to David Garrick, the great Shakespearean actor, and later to Sara Siddons, who virtually created the role of

Angelica Kauffman, of herself hesitating between the arts of music and painting. (By kind permission of Major the Rt. Hon. Lord St. Oswald M.C., D.L., of Nostell Priority.)

Lady Macbeth, typecasting it for future generations of actresses. Other friends included Madam Vigée-Lebrun, another very famous woman artist and court painter to Marie Antoinette. The two women painters became friends and "sisters," as Vigée-Lebrun referred to their friendship.

In addition to the hundreds of portraits executed by Kauffman of people from all over Europe, her work was the direct inspiration for biscuit porcelain which was modeled by J. J. Spangler, a Swiss. Angelica's paintings were used as the decorative motifs on porcelain produced in the Worcester, Derby, and Swansea potteries, as well as the potteries of Sevres and Meissen. These works were executed by such

"Sara Siddons," G. Stuart. (National Portrait Gallery, London)

masters of their craft as Thomas Baxter, John Brewer, and Humphrey Chamberlain. Scenes from her pictures constantly were reproduced, for in addition to portraits, she executed many paintings using the classical motifs so popular during her time. There are two very fine examples of English Derby porcelain at the Victoria and Albert Museum in London which exemplifies her influence. (If one is lucky, and willing to look, examples of her porcelain can still be discovered in antique shops throughout England, for as yet, she has not experienced a revival, although with the renewed interest in women's work there is a strong indication that her work will begin to be sought and prices will soar.)

Two examples of porcelain inspired by Kauffman's work. (Österreichisches Museum fur angewandte Kunst, Wein)

Angelica Kauffman of herself. (National Portrait
Gallery, London)

Syon House interior. Designed by Robert Adam.
(By gracious permission of His Grace, the Duke of
Northumberland, England)

The popular color print was another area in which Angelica Kauffman was influential. (These prints can still be
purchased throughout Britain, and the thrill of discovering
one is beyond words.) Among the leading engravers of the
day was William Ryland, who introduced the "chalk manner" of engraving to England. Francesco Bartolozzi, engraver, etcher, stipple engraver, and painter was also a
friend, and executed many of her paintings into engravings.
The idea of painting or engraving becoming standardized,
repeatable, or mechanical and all other negative implications
which have become associated with mass-produced art did
not exist; mechanization and standardization were seen as
instruments of democracy by the newly emerging English
middle class. These prints eventually found their way into
collections throughout England, Europe and the United
States. Probably more of the common folk were familiar
with Angelica's work than that of any other artist of the
time.

"The Artist in the Character of Design Listening to the Inspiration of Poetry," Angelica Kauffman. (The Greater London Council as Trustees of the Iveagh Bequest, Kenwood, England)

In England, Kauffman's work can best be seen at the National Gallery, the National Portrait Gallery, and the Victoria and Albert Museum. Her decorative work can be seen in some of England's most beautiful and stately homes. To truly enjoy and experience the eighteenth century's "Grand Manner," one should visit the many homes designed by the architect Robert Adam, and filled with decorative work created by Adam's team of craftsmen, including work by Angelica and her husband, Antonio Zucchi.

Later in her life, Angelica met and married Antonio Zucchi, a decorative painter as her father had been. Before she married, however, Angelica and Antonio drew up a mar-

Syon House interior. Designed by Robert Adam.
(By gracious permission of His Grace, the Duke of
Northumberland)

riage contract which stated that all the money Angelica made
was hers, and hers alone. She also decided to retain her
maiden name, but later she decided to add Zucchi's name to
hers. Some of her later work was signed "Kauffman-Zucchi."
It was Antonio who encouraged her to complete some decorative work for the architect Robert Adam. Antonio was a
decorative painter and made less than half the income that
Angelica did from portrait commissions. He later became her
agent, devoting the remainder of his life to her promotion,
care, and business contracts. He even entertained her clients
and generally freed her to concentrate on just her painting.

Kauffman's work is probably most accessible through
the interior decor of the Robert Adam homes in England.
Adam was a pioneer who led the way to a complete trans-
formation of Georgian design. His clients were all the
wealthy and aristocratic citizens of England. Angelica joined
Adam's entourage of master craftsmen in 1776. Her paint-

Mantelpiece by Angelica Kauffman. In Courtauld Home, designed by Robert Adam, London. (*Angelica Kauffman, Her Life and Works,* G. C. Williamson and Lady Victoria Manners. The Bodley Head Publishers, London, England)

ings, with their classic themes and color, complemented magnificently Adam's interiors, for the colors that were used by Adam tended toward pastel shades (pale greens and pinks) which were predominant in fabrics and wall coverings. A very fine example among many of Adam's work can be found at the building at twenty Portman Square, London, now known as the Courtauld Institute of Art, open and affiliated with the University of London. In addition, Kauffman's work can be seen at the Royal Academy, in the ceiling decorative motifs.

In 1783 Angelica returned to Rome where she continued to paint until her death in 1807. Her funeral was held in

Rome, and was recorded at that time as the largest to ever pass through the streets. The entire membership of the Royal Academy of England was in attendance and the first four directors of the Academy walked at the four corners of her pall, while two academicians held up two of her paintings which caught and reflected the glimmering candlelight from the hundreds of lighted tapers carried by the aristocracy and the famous of England and Europe. The eulogy for Kauffman echoed through the church: "Hail! Most Excellent Woman and in Peace, Farewell, Mother of all the Arts."

Her bust was later placed in the Pantheon in Rome. Historians have chosen to remember Angelica Kauffman as a "minor decorative painter." Her decorative work was indeed "minor," but only in relationship to her other fine portraits and paintings, and because decorative painting is a field where women have always been allowed to excel. Angelica Kauffman was, indeed, deserving of a greater tribute. Her contemporaries honored her and respected her; it is *his*-tory that has relegated her and her achievement.

Marble bust of Angelica Kauffman. (Musei Capi-
tolini, Rome)

500 Years of
Birth in Art Forms—
No One Gives a Damn!

Men have carefully preserved "man's" heritage through the establishment of museums—museums that house everything from cars, engines, planes, trains, spacecraft, memorabilia of war and destruction to "man's" contributions in the arts and crafts. Not only have women's contributions in the arts been overlooked, but our contributions to Western civilization's sciences and industry as well. Everything that is associated with the female of the species had to take second place in competion with male-oriented ideas of what is important enough to carefully record for future generations. Included with this oversight is a lack of interest in the process of propagating civilization itself—birth. As women, we have been so 'ghettoized' by our wombs, that we are isolated from a part of history that affects us as well as men. Because of the lack of information concerning birth, many women have had to suffer needlessly. Although a great deal of controversy surrounds the subject of birth today, most of the discussion focuses not on birth, but on who controls our bodies—us or society? Reference to birth has always been coated with overly sentimental ideas connected with motherhood, foisted on us by a patriarchal society that hoped to "keep us in our place" by romanticizing, but at the same time devaluing, parenthood. In the process, we lost control of what is essentially our rights over our own bodies, including the practice of helping each other out during birth. Midwifery was replaced by big-money business and male-dominated gynecology, which in turn dispersed information to us on the intellectual level of a prepuberty textbook on sex and hygiene, and offered about the same amount of emotional support as well.

Fortunately, a handful of enlightened sisters started women's health centers and even published books complete with actual illustrations of birth. Our right of watching and participating in our own labor and giving birth had also been denied to us—we were strapped down to the table and drugged out of our minds.

It is no wonder then, that birth iconography in artwork is obviously lacking in our twentieth century images. Unlike our prehistoric sisters and "primitive" women in backwoods areas throughout the world, we never experienced birth, even though we had given birth. The most dramatic moment in our lives was denied to us, controlled as it were, by the male-dominated medical field. Woman's body is still, even today, considered shameful, and the idea of watching a birth on television is strongly censored with "adult warnings" for viewers. Mary Wollstonecraft, although she lived in the eighteenth century, long before our "liberated" views on the subject, also made a plea to women concerning their bodies. She said: "It would be proper to familiarize the sexes to an unreserved discussion of those topics which are generally avoided in conversation from a principle of false delicacy; and that it would be right to speak of the organs of generation as freely as we mention our eyes or our hands." Her plea went unheard and she herself eventually died giving birth to her daughter, Mary Shelley.

Figures of pregnant women abound in primitive cultures and are found all over the world in archaeological digs. Women in the process of giving birth was a rich source of iconography used by primitive cultures. Examples can be found in paintings on pre-Columbian pottery of women in the squatting position of birth. This squatting position, so familiar to primitive women for birthing, is thought to be a revolutionary new method of giving birth today as many of our hospitals are now using a bed-chair device that allows the woman to sit up while bearing the baby. According to primitive art however, this is nothing new at all. If our history as women had been better recorded, women today would realize that many of the 'modern' methods of giving birth were practiced by almost every civilization since prehistoric days.

I have been fortunate to see a collection of birthing devices and art objects connected with birth dating back to medieval times, but unfortunately you will not have this opportunity, for these works have no place among our museum collections. I refer to the "Womanhood Collection" of Trude Collison Baxter.

In a tiny Essex English village called Thaxted, Trude Collison Baxter has dedicated the past thirty years of her life to a collection which deals with all facets of birth and birth iconography. I first heard of this woman when I was in England and read about her collection in an editorial written by the English feminist, Dora Russell. I was interested, but it was only after my return to the United States in 1976 that Trude Collison Baxter and I began our lengthy correspondence. Her life was spent in the village as a midwife. Over the years she has collected furniture, paintings and prints of early birth scenes, books, equipment of all kinds relating to midwifery, early baby clothes and documents. Her collection is interesting, for among the many objects is a medieval 'birthing chair' dating from 1400. In this beautifully hand-

Medieval birth chair, circa 1400. Shown here as used in wealthy English homes, covered with plush velvet cushions. The woman sat comfortably on this chair until her water broke, then the chair was made ready for delivery. The chair is comfortable, with sturdy arm rests, which give a great deal of support—unlike the metal sides of most contemporary hospital beds. Trude Baxter collection, Thaxted, England. (Photograph by Robert W. Ott)

Medieval birth chair, shown here without velvet
cushions and seat removed. Note the detailed
carving. Trude Baxter collection. (Photograph by
Robert Ott)

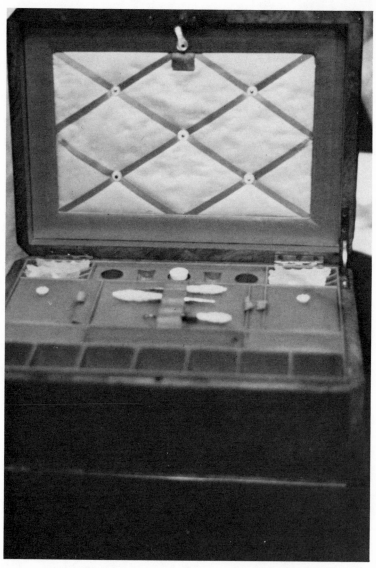

An early sewing box used to make baby clothes.
Trude Baxter collection. (Photograph by Robert
Ott)

carved chair sat the woman in labor. When the baby was ready to be born, the bottom of the chair lifted out in a large crescent shape and the baby was delivered into the arms of the midwife. She has also collected an assortment of prints and books dealing with Greek images of birth, including accounts of Socrates as the son of a well-known midwife and Hippocrates and his accounts and observances of birth cases, including obstetrics of the time.

In addition to the printed material and art reproductions, there is a fine group of actual pieces including the medieval birth chair. She has also collected straw-filled linen cushions which were used during birth and then destroyed; a delicately-sewn and crafted hood cover for a baby cot brought to England by the Crusaders; an actual handcrafted baby cot dating from 1350; a midwife's oak cupboard for cord strings, and a thirteenth century baby feeding cup made of horn. Also included is a hand-carved facsimile of a baby used during the eighteenth century in the training of midwives.

In 1977, my husband, daughter, and I decided to visit Trude while staying in London for a few weeks. We discovered there was no direct route to her small Essex village from London, but we managed to find a train that would get us more than halfway there. After changing at a place called Bishop Stortford, we continued on our journey to the town of Elsenham. Upon disembarking at Elsenham it was another thirty-five minutes through isolated, but beautiful, farmlands of Essex. As our little car (driven by an amicable village man whom Trude had asked to meet us) wound slowly around the rolling isolated hills, hugging the road, I soon became aware of the necessity of a midwife so far from any major town. Our driver referred to Trude Collison Baxter however, as "Mrs. Baker," the only name he said he knew her by.

As fate would have it, Trude was on the edge of defeat and desperation concerning her collection. She had applied to various institutions for financial help in preserving it, but was flatly turned down. Most male administrators of these institutions thought she was, in her own words, "a total nut case" for wanting to preserve a collection that dealt with "motherhood" and "womanhood." So, our trip to see her, coming as we did, all the way from the United States to her door in an isolated Essex village, certainly must have seemed to her like fate, or the province, in this case, of a divine goddess. At any rate, we soon arrived and were greeted by a warm, delightfully maternal-looking woman.

Trude immediately cleared up the "Mrs. Baker/Mrs. Baxter" name business by informing us when she separated, or as she put it, "got shuck" of Mr. Baker, her husband, she decided to take on the feminine equivalent of a baker which is a baxter.

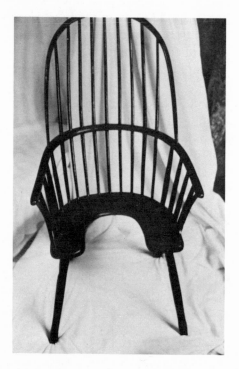

An 18th century birth chair. Trude Baxter collection. (Photograph by Robert Ott)

Medieval birth chair with the seat removed and midwife's stool in place. The midwife sat on the stool and literally caught the baby as it was delivered. Trude Baxter collection. (Photograph by Robert Ott)

She also changed her middle name to her grandmother's surname of Collison, for as Trude said: "My grandmother was the only woman in the family who had a good marriage." With this marvelous feminist introduction we got to work photographing and talking about her collection. I was delighted to learn that in addition to being a qualified midwife and lecturer on midwifery at the local university, Trude Collison Baxter also held a diploma in art. I hadn't known this before, but upon seeing the valuable collection, realized that it was someone with the educated eye of an artist who had chosen these exquisite works of art dealing with birth iconography.

She lives in only one room of her large house, the house itself dating back many centuries. The rest of the rooms of the house are devoted to the collection, each piled high with boxes, carefully catalogued and meticulously protected by covers and sheets. My husband, an art professor specializing in museum education, became astounded as he photographed one rare piece after another, whispering to me, "You'll never again be so physically close to such valuable antiques and artifacts as you are now, except in a museum." It was then perhaps that the knowledge dawned on me how truly dedicated this woman had been for the past thirty years, believing in the importance of woman's *her*-story. Although in need of money to eat, and simply more room in

Trude Baxter with "midwife's cabinet," circa 1700. This cabinet was always well-stocked with cord ties, knotted linen and other necessary birthing equipment. Trude Baxter collection. (Photograph by Robert Ott)

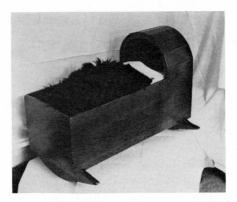

A 15th century English oak baby cot. Note the low
hood protecting the baby from drafts. The bear-
skin blanket was considered to have magical
powers. A cot such as this would be found only in
homes where the newborn was expected to immediately reflect the aristocracy of its parents. Trude
Baxter collection. (Photograph by Robert Ott)

which to live, she never sold one piece to break up the collection, believing firmly that to do so would ruin the consisten-
cy of the entire collection. Instead she has held on, sacrificing
her own comfort in order that one day women will be able to
see a chronologically visual presentation of the *her*-story of
birth. She has maintained strong convictions concerning her
collection and its importance, even when confronted with
ridicule. She has maintained her philosophy, and as she told
my daughter:

> Birth, being the creation of all civilization, comes down
> like a great crystal triangle circling around from age to
> age with thousands of facets on it, with all different
> kinds and types of human beings resting on one point—
> and that is birth. The tragedy of all human history, I
> have found while researching childbirth, is that all the
> sorrow and miseries of the world are because we do not
> evaluate birth to the degree and give it the primary posi-
> tion it should have in all civilization. Birth, really, in all

its process, is as beautiful as all other artistic achievements, and should be viewed as natural rather than a "sickness." Unfortunately for many women, birth is not beautiful because of the misery, poverty, shame and degradation into which so much of the human race is born. Many times, unfortunately, women are used as human factories for producing wage earners and as sort of corporation slaves within marriage where true partnership is not really established.

When we had finished our recording and photographing of the collection, Trude surprised us with a marvelous dinner, one which she obviously had unselfishly been preparing for quite some time. Her joy in finding someone who shared her views and enthusiasm was contagious and she obviously went all out for our celebration of meeting—uncorking the wine and toasting the day and our friendship.

Chippendale baby cot, circa 1790. Trude Baxter collection. (Photograph by Robert Ott)

A cast iron baby cot, showing the influence of the Industrial Revolution in England. The basket is handmade, with Gothic decorated feet. Trude Baxter collection. (Photograph by Robert Ott)

A 15th century oak midwife's stool, restored, showing binder used by midwife to position the baby. Trude Baxter collection. (Photograph by Robert Ott)

When it was time to leave, Trude accompanied us to the little train station. As our train pulled slowly away from the village, we waved and waved to her, a solitary, lonely figure standing firmly on the empty platform and her words echoed in my head: "If I just hang on long enough someone will see my viewpoint."

There is a wealth of female iconography to be found in birth for the artist. As women artists become aware of their own rich experiences in life as women, when women artists create from those experiences, instead of prostituting their vision so that they will be accepted by the male-controlled art world, when women, as well as men, find relevance in all aspects of their lives, then we will see this reflected in ourselves, our environment, and the images we are creating. As

Dora Russell wrote in her editorial which led me to Trude Collison Baxter: "Motherhood is glamorized and romanticized and at the same time undervalued. Should we not ask what is the meaning of the march of tens of thousands of women in defense of the hard won reform of the abortion law? I agree entirely with their protests; but why are women marching against children instead of for them? Our technological society is actively inimical to them, and women becoming aware of this—as of the population explosion—increasingly reject childbearing. Yet in children, not electronics, lies our survival."

Unfortunately, as of this writing, no museum or collection has responded to Trude Collison Baxter's or Dora Russell's appeal to preserve this collection. Eventually various pieces from this collection will probably appear in fragmented collections, for Trude will be forced to either disperse it, or it will be dispersed after her death; she, in that eventuality, will never see the realization of her dream. No one in our technological and male-oriented society cares enough. It is a collection, at the moment, no one gives a damn about.

Dialogue with a
Craftswoman

Chloe Dellaport is an artist who makes babies—clay babies. She lives in an isolated area in the center of Pennsylvania and has not been particularly involved with the feminist movement or feminist art. I first discovered her work at a small exhibition at a local college in Pennsylvania. I was impressed and curiously interested in her "babies," for I saw something in their images that spoke of a reality that perhaps had not been seen in previous work using infants as subjects. Her little creatures had a life all their own, and were not shrouded in overly sentimental, mythological meanings.

Throughout history there have been paintings and sculptures of babies. One need only look at the Baroque period to see significant portrayal of infants—infants with fat round bottoms, and cherub faces, wings sprouting from their backs. They always represented "purity" and "preciousness." Even today babies smile out at us from contemporary greeting cards. They are portrayed as overly sweet, painted in pastel pinks and blues, the colors as stereotyped as their images.

On the other hand, Chloe Dellaport's "babies" are created from her experience as a woman and mother. Gone is the "preciousness" in her forms. Her work and her words reveal a sensitive person, and her work reflects a woman creating from a rich female experience, unintimidated by her materials and chosen theme of imagery.

How did you happen to start creating ceramic babies?

I would like to say that it was some big inspiration, but I really don't think it was. I had been wanting to start something new and I always liked figures. Of course I got into ceramics through sculpture, and since I like figures—human beings—I wanted to make people out of clay. I thought of making parts and putting them down on a surface, and arranging them. And then I can't remember how the baby thing came, whether I made this little head and suddenly said, ". . . this little baby . . . babies would be interesting to make . . ." This was just how it started.

There is so much you can say about babies. I really consciously tried to seek out our [women's] relationship to babies, and express all kinds of different things that had to do with babies. The abortion thing that's in everyone's heads had a little bit to do with it, and the killing in Vietnam . . . I was also interested in the big generalities about babies, you know, the "preciousness" of babies and the sentimentality that people attach to babyhood. Then the reality of how they actually affect you comes through. Each time I began working, I would start out with this general idea of what I had in mind to do and as I worked the idea might change its meaning. In one incident, the piece didn't really give its whole meaning to me until I was practically finished and was "dressing" it. It started out with just a head. I made it and it was too pretty, so I put it in a salt kiln, and it came out looking "weathered." The baby came out of the kiln having a wonderful kind of weathered look, and I started thinking of it as an old image, an icon. I was putting this velvet collar on

"Cupid as Captive," Francois Boucher. In the Baroque period, babies represented purity and preciousness, with fat round bottoms, cherubic faces, and wings sprouting from their backs. (Crown Copyright)

it, and a hat, and I was thinking of altar ladies in a church. I was thinking dolls, babies, and dressing them was going through my head. It is hard to explain the feeling you get when doing that.

Who or what was the greatest influence on your work?

I would say that no one artist, certainly my experience with dolls as a child comes into my work. I loved dolls when I was a little girl, and my mother said, "It seems you haven't outgrown it." Of course, I had never thought of them as just "dolls," and someone said something about me and my "dolls," I was almost insulted, it was demeaning somehow.

Why do you become disturbed when people refer to them as "dolls"?

It's the old thing, you think you're creating art; it's something more dimensional than a toy.

Actually, don't you think artists are all children, that we haven't really outgrown our curiosity, and the ability to explore new possibilities?

Certainly, but sometimes that creative experience is channeled into other areas.

Why do babies interest you so much?

There are so many different facets to it. First, they are just fun to do. I like throwing on the wheel, and I love forming the parts out of these wheel things—you know, the potter's wheel. It's really interesting to combine these thrown pieces, and when you make the features and you stick your hands in the inside and push out the cheeks and features—it's really a fantastic experience, and fun. I like working. When I work with these little babies, I really enjoy it.

Statuette of a naked, crying child. Dates back to the pre-Aztec civilization. Note the similarity of Dellaport's babies to this pre-Aztec baby. Both are depicted honestly, without over-sentimentality. (*The World of the Aztecs*, William Prescott. Tudor Publishing, New York. Photograph by Giraudon.)

Did you ever feel intimidated because you were creating baby images? Did you ever feel that perhaps you were a woman and maybe you shouldn't be creating an image that so many women want to disassociate themselves with because "babies" have been used to "ghettoize" us as women?

No, art being what it is today, I've never felt intimidated. I've always gone my own way, but once in a while I would be told by some people that I was neurotic because I created only "baby" images. Some people even suggested that I might be in need of professional help.

Chloe Dellaport, craftswoman.

Clay babies by Chloe Dellaport. (Hoffa collection)

I've noticed that your work is in series.

The training I had in college did not make a point about pressing and investigating one particular idea. Working in a series is a wonderful way to work. With these babies, I had so many things I wanted to do and say, I just stuck with them, working out various ideas.

What is the symbolism, do you feel, in your images? You have already mentioned the "preciousness" syndrome. Any others?

I would like to think that they have all kinds of meanings. I would rather think that their meanings are ambiguous. It takes on new dimension when you go back and look at a piece, and you see if from day to day and look and respond to it differently.

Detail of clay babies.

What are some other interpretations you have received?

I think people look at them and everyone gets a different feeling and a different interpretation. For an example: I had a
group of "babies" in a group women's exhibit. They were
viewed in the context of "war babies." I had no intention of
them being "war babies." I could see how they could think of
them as war babies though. However, the one piece that I did
create about the Vietnam war was an arrangement of babies
on a green board. It was like a game, you know, the babies
were lying on a game board—one was scarred up too. But I
thought that was interesting, that a group of babies would be
considered as "war babies" when, in fact, I did not have that
in mind for the particular piece that was in the women's exhibition.

There was one piece that had a baby in a tissue box.
That could be interpreted as something to do with abortion.
People that are for woman's right to make her own decision

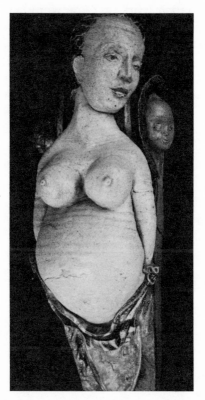

"Rachel," pregnant masthead with babies by Chloe Dellaport. (Photograph by Jeanne Stevens-Sollman)

would feel that this was indicating a waste of children, putting the baby in a Kleenex box, where as the people that were against abortion might think that children are being disposed of—putting them in a Kleenex box like trash. So the same piece can evoke a different response. I don't mind this at all, as long as it evokes some kind of response.

Your work seems to come from your experience as a woman. Is this true?

I would say that there are certain images, shapes, ideas, that women put into their work that you wouldn't find in a man's work. A man came up to me after an exhibit—and it was the way he talked to me—he was so sympathetic in the way that he felt. I think men do respond to the babies differently than women, in a way, yes, I do. I also think I work from my experience as a woman, a mother, whatever. Artists all work from their individual experiences, don't they?

Creativity—Procreativity

The students enrolled in an introductory dance class in a university physical education course had visited an exhibition of drawings and were asked to react to the exhibit through dance. A videotape had been made of the students' reactions, and now they were preparing to view the results.

They entered the dance studio and sat down informally on the floor, some talking, others involved in individual exercise movements as they waited for the videotape to begin. For these students, viewing their movements on videotape was nothing new. The one difference in this otherwise routine situation was that sitting among them, unknown, was the artist whose work they had studied and interpreted. They were now about to see the results on the video screen. The room darkened and as the tape started, everyone became silent. The blue light of the screen flickered across some twenty anticipating faces. There was no sound or music to accompany the tape, silence filled the room, adding an unusual quality to the atmosphere as we watched the slow, unfolding, undulating movements of dancers on the set.

The exhibition that these students had reacted to was a series of some twenty graphite drawings depicting organic

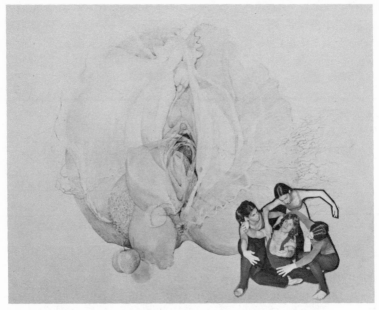

"Labyrinth to Re-Birth," Joelynn Snyder-Ott. Interpreted through dance by members of the Contemporary Dance Company, Pennsylvania State
University.

and female body art combined with the theme of birth/re-
birth. The drawings were filled with intricate linear detail,
many lines weaving in and around the forms. Images of pods
or womb-like forms predominated in the drawings which
used fruit as a metaphor—seeds rolling from vulnerable
tender-like centers.

The class had been divided into groups of four or five
dancers, and some groups seemed to interpret the drawings
as a whole, others reacted to individual drawings. Perhaps it
was a combination of the darkness of the room, and the ab-
solute silence and concentration of the class as they watched
their movements, but the overall effect was that of participating, seeing in fact, some ancient primordial dance with
the dancers opening and closing against each other, moving

in and around, creating forms that occasionally would split open, a dancer rolling in a ball, out from between parted limbs—not unsimilar to the imagery in the drawings of the seed rolling away from the pit of the fruit. Some of the dancers reacted to the membranous lines of the drawings, interpreting their suggestive forms by circling other dancers, weaving in and around through the group, their arms undulating in rapid rhythm, reinterpreting the imagery expressed in the drawings.

I, as the artist, found this to be an experience of deep emotion. First, it was moving to see young student dancers (students who were neither professional dancers nor artists) reacting so deeply and almost identically, at least visually, to what I had felt when creating the works. I was seeing two-dimensional forms, "my" content, lines and form, as it were, coming to life as a three-dimensional reality. The drawings were literally lifted from the surface and given breathing life through the interpretations of these young students. The experience was intense, rather similar to a *déjà vu* of some ancient activity, not unsimilar, I imagined, to fertility rites practiced long before the coming of patriarchal religions, and the subsequent suppression of female sexuality.

At the end of the videotape, the instructor introduced me to the class as the artist whose work they had seen and studied for this exercise. The students were all quite eager to ask questions and share their emotions concerning the interpretive problem of reacting to an art form outside their discipline. A male student related that viewing an art exhibit in order to interpret it through dance had forced him to experience the exhibit—seeing forms and lines that, as he said, he most probably would have overlooked in just a "viewing" situation. He had been filled with a great deal of emotion, both in viewing the exhibit, and also in dancing out its content and forms.

Since the thrust of the exhibit was birth, we talked about the fertility theme, and how fertility was treated in ancient religions, as compared to later patriarchal religions. In the ancient religions, women in many ways always predominated, a natural phenomenon in a strong matriarchal society. In ancient Sumerian and Egyptian religions, particular emphasis was placed on plant fertility, and since my drawings had a great deal of organic as well as plant imagery, perhaps the dancers' response was based on an ancient primordial collective unconscious. In the later religions of Judaism and Christianity, sexuality was not deemed a virtue and the female principle was often altogether absent. The drawings represented, with symbolic imagery from the Great Mother era, woman as an active participant in the great birth, death and resurrection mystery. The students were sharing with me, the artist, in an experience that predated the New Testament, for by the time the books of the New Testament were written, women had become a symbolic rather than an active

"Venus of Laussel," circa 15,000-10,000, B.C. (Musee d'Aquitaine, Bordeaux, France)

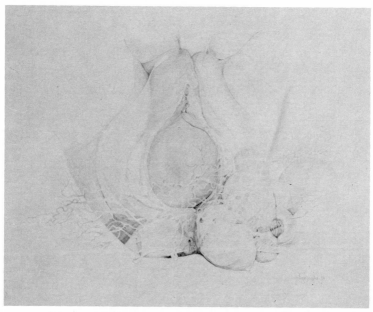

"Among the Roots, Golden Threads are Glistening." ("Joie de Vivre" series), Joelynn Snyder-Ott, graphite drawing.

participant in the great death and resurrection mystery. In later religions, fertility is spiritual rather than physical. In my drawings, fertility is physical, alive, and belonging to the woman.

In my drawings were images of fruit, vegetation and other organic forms which we discussed. We talked about the fertility myth of Mesopotamia and how the Great Mother goddess descended from the paleolithic moon goddess of an earlier age. This great mother, called *Inanna* by Sumerians and *Ishtar* by Semitic invaders, represented earth, love, and fertility. Her mate was *Dumuzi* or *Tanmuz*, a vegetation god descended from earlier gods. As Mesopotamian religions became increasingly patriarchal, the Great Mother was relegated to second-class status together with the great sky gods and their sacred sons. The ancient Egyptians placed special emphasis on fertility, perhaps because of their location in a fertile river valley. The Phrygians worshiped one of the great Great Mothers, Cybele, and in India, archaeological evidence indicates the Great Mother cult was the earliest, just as matriarchal cults were antecedent to the patriarchal mythologies of Mesopotamia, Egypt, and Greece.

The young dance students had reacted to the drawings aesthetically, but also and perhaps more importantly— sometimes overlooked by most teachers and art historians— they reacted at a deeper consciousness level, a consciousness level filled with emotion connecting them to each other, and each to the artist, and all to a universal awareness, an awareness that was neither matriarchal nor patriarchal but perhaps a combination of the two, reflecting purpose and continuity. We found from this experience that even when the matriarchal element has been suppressed by patriarchal religion, the female will eventually emerge because of natural human instinct toward a balanced view of existence. The Chinese express this balance of polarities as *yin* and *yang* (yin as the feminine, and yang as the masculine). Christian religions express these polarities by the assumption of the Virgin Mother Mary and Jesus, and in India, the marriage of Shiva and Parvati.

Eventually we presented the dance interpretation and art program to members of the local chapter of the American Association of University Women, taking our "related arts program" to the public, as it were. Participating in this particular program were members of the Pennsylvania State University professional dance company under the direction of Patricia Heigel-Tanner. The program was set up so that the audience (which included a cross section of the general public, art students, and members of the chapter) would react to the drawings at exactly the same time as the dancers. The professional dancers had never seen the artwork and would see it only simultaneously with the audience. We told the audience what was to take place, but did not burden them with a great deal of pre-program rhetoric. We asked the audience to participate too by either writing down their initial reaction to the artwork, or to get up and join in with the dancers if they were so moved.

The dancers walked around the center of the room to obtain the "feel" of the dancing surface and space. We had organized the chairs in a circle around the open space where the dancers would be working. After becoming familiar with the space, the dancers signaled they were ready. We showed the entire group of drawings on a large screen, and then we turned on the lights exposing the actual drawings which were placed against the wall of the room. The audience was invited to get up and view the actual works if they so desired.

After about fifteen minutes the first slide was projected onto the screen and the dancers began to move rhythmically together. Slowly, the drawing became the dancers, and the dancers became the living organic moving forms of the drawing. The audience was spellbound; the only sound in the room was the occasional "squish" of the bare foot of a dancer. Many people in the audience began to write immediately, others sat as if hypnotized by the slow gyrating movements of the dancers against the backdrop of the drawings, creating a living art form—moving, grouping, and reforming.

At the end of the program, everyone was eager to share the experience, the descriptive adjectives they had scribbled down, and to engage the dancers, as well as me, in what became a very interesting dialogue, and an intense evening—an evening that had perhaps brought new insights and more meaningful art awareness, as well as a heightened consciousness level to a group of people who, as some later expressed, had no idea they could ever respond to a work of art as dramatically and with such strong emotions.

For me, as the artist, this experience was validating and positive. As I watched "my" forms and lines come alive through the dance movement, I couldn't resist the impulse to want to share the same experience with my own drawing

Contemporary African fertility figure from Durban, South Africa. Note the similarity in form and design of this contemporary African fertility figure to the ancient Egyptian ankh which evolved later into the Christian cross. Is the cross, then, a "female" symbol upon which the son of God was sacrificed, perpetuating the ancient sacrificial ritual of bloodletting over the earth as an imitation of the menstrual blood, which to the ancients, was a sign of fertility? If woman was fertile because she bled, then would the earth, also, become fertile if drenched with sacrifical blood? To the ancients, these sacrifices were carried out in the spring, to insure a "rebirth" of fertile crops. To Christians, the "passion" of Christ at Easter is a symbol of rebirth. In essence, both represent the same thing. (Snyder collection)

Prehistoric Great Mother from Senorbi. Note the similarity in form between this ancient fertility figure, the contemporary African fertility figure, and the subsequent likeness to the later Christian cross.

students. How exciting for them to be able to see their own artistic efforts on paper come alive, validating their experience, their work, and their feelings. Even the simplest line drawing can take on movement and create an interesting statement, a direction, and feeling, when interpreted through another discipline such as dance or music. As I watched the dancers, my mind was racing ahead, thinking of other possibilities of sharing such a related art experience. "Next time," I thought, "we'll combine organic sounds of nature such as water, the wind, or other yin-oriented music deriving directly from the earth, without any emphasis on technology-produced sounds, keeping the entire experience female or yin in juxtaposition to yang or masculine-oriented ideas."

We chose the theme of birth/rebirth as our subject, for

indeed that was the thrust of the content of the drawings in the series. The theme of birth/rebirth affects us all, and as Lucy Lippard stated in a recent article in *Art News*, "The Pains and Pleasures of Rebirth: Women's Body Art": "Perhaps procreativity is the next taboo to be tackled in art." We feel that we've made that attempt. The theme is nothing new, we only have to reexamine the ancient past to find a wealth of material just waiting to be rediscovered. Sharing art with artists in another medium, seeing their reaction to a work of art using all their creative faculties is a personal *joie de vivre*. Becoming involved in an art form with one's whole being, one's total sense of sight, hearing, movement through feeling, and finally one's intuitive, as well as logical, thought processes is a liberating and fantastically exciting experience.

An Art School for Women

In 1972 at a small women's art college, I interviewed students and faculty about attitudes and training, role models, and the relationship between male and female faculty members. Total enrollment in this college is about four hundred women students. It was not my goal to deal in statistics, but rather to present a cross section of young women from various departments, letting them speak for themselves. The students were enrolled in the departments of textile design, fashion design, art education, photography, and advertising design. I was particularly interested in this college as a former graduate.

Why did you choose to come to a women's art college instead of a coed art school, or university art department?

I wanted to study with all girls. The concentration is better. You don't have to worry all the time how you look, you know, the whole cosmetic thing.

When you have guys in the class there is distraction, and also the girls are always trying to prove themselves.

Do you mean, you feel that you have to prove yourself constantly when you are in a class with male students?

Yes. I came here, you see, because I thought it was more of a professional school—that I would get more personal attention because it was so small, and the fact that this school is not coed really wasn't on my mind when I was thinking about choosing it. I guess I feel now, that when I work, I work, and I don't care who is around.

Why did you come here instead of attending a university?

Well, I think you get lost in a university. This is a professional kind of place. The people who are around you here, all the time, are artists too. I think an art school has more creative energy than a university art department. I also think that it's important to be located in a large city—something can be said for a city and the kind of creative energy that it creates.

What do you hope to have gained by your four years here?

I think that I will have gained knowledge, more creativity, a better feeling about myself. I should feel better about myself.

Yes, good, but that has to do with your emotions—which is fine, but in a more practical sense: How do you expect to "eat" when you graduate from here? This is supposed to be a school that trains women for positions in the art world—at least that was how it began.

I came here so that I could eventually get a job in my chosen field, but I know a lot of other girls who are here only to meet a guy.

I'm not here to meet a man, or to just get a degree and that's it. I know that I will have a whole lot more to learn when I leave here. What I mean is, it is not an end to my learning process. If that were the case, then I shouldn't be here at all.

None of you have mentioned a career, but rather you keep referring to "getting a job." Is there a difference?

I hadn't thought much about that. I guess a job is something that seems temporary until something better comes along, but a career, well, that sounds like your entire life.

I hope to learn a craft here, so that my craft will support me while I go into the fine arts. In that sense, I guess I would consider the craft stuff as a job while the painting part would be my career.

You seem to think there is a big division between the crafts and the fine arts?

I still think you get the feeling, at least here, that the crafts aren't as important as the fine arts. Maybe someday they will both be as important as each other. Some of the things you see now in the galleries are stitchery stuff and craft kinds of things—things that a lot of people are calling fine art when in reality they're crafts, crafts that women have been doing for a long time. Like my grandmother for instance, she was always making quilts. Now you go to a museum, and you see them hanging there. It really makes you wonder.

Sometimes I wonder who decides what is fine art and what isn't.

Many times we hear that women's schools are heavy on social life and light on the work. Is that true, in all honesty?

No.

No, that's really so untrue.

You can't have too much social life here, freshmen year especially. The work is so hard. They weed out the girls who don't make it with the work and the assignments.

There are a few girls who do just enough to get by, but they are in such a minority. A lot of girls come out of high school, and a lot of them come here because they think it's "fun and games," and after the first year they realize what they have to do, and they either get out or they stay and work like hell. The ones who came to play, aren't here anymore. They weed them out.

What would you say is the ratio of male instructors here at this women's art school?

About half and half.

Art education is the exception. There are more female instructors in art education.

What about the other fields—the fine-arts studio courses?

Well, now that I think of it like that, I would have to say there are more male teachers than female.

All the department heads are men with the exception of art education and textile design.

What would you say is the strongest department here?

Probably advertising design.

The painting department is strong too.

Is the art history instructor male or female?

We have three instructors, two female and one male.

That leads me to a very important question. As women art students, how many other women artists have you studied in art history courses?

None.

None, I can't remember any. No, we never studied any that I can remember.

Well, I remember Mary Cassatt, but that's all.

Doesn't that seem strange to you?

I honestly never thought about it, but now that you've mentioned it, my God! that's really right.

What art history text are you using?

Janson's *Art History.* [Janson's *Art History* text is used in almost every U.S. Art Appreciation course and Basic Art History. There are *no women artists* included.]

I remember one of our instructors pointed out to us that many of the women who created long ago signed their work with men's names.

You know, I'm just sitting here wondering why we never have studied anything about women artists. We studied all about male artists, but their subjects were always women.

With all these male instructors, do you think you are developing as women and as individuals, or are you being forced to see the world as men see it without taking into account your vision as women?

You refer to them as male, and the way I feel about it is that they are instructors. I think of them as people. If an instructor happens to be male, and he has some kind of a chauvinist attitude, that's his problem, and he'll always be that way, but if he is like a normal person, and respects the rights of everyone then this is fine, and he's not influencing me in any way with male values.

I think, if anything, a lot of male instructors, and even some of our female instructors, try to make you more masculine—that is they stress strength in line, color, and everything. Painting very lightly, for example, is out, or using pastel shades or something like that.

Well, that's still their problem, and it will always be their problem.

Yeah! but you are a strong person, and you are aware of this, but what about some of us who are afraid to speak up?

Look, I'm sure there are plenty of female instructors who give male students a hard time at other schools.

Maybe it really doesn't have to do with the instructor's sex at all. There are plenty of female art instructors that are indoctrinated by male values, and they are passing them on to us too. Those are the kind of women who say it's a real compliment to be told you "paint like a man," or something like that.

There are certain men faculty members who are very strong as instructors, and a lot of women are afraid to stand up to them. It's the old father image thing. You wouldn't go against your father, but you would go against your mother—at least in Jewish homes it's like that.

Whom do you take more seriously when it comes to a critique of your work—male or female instructors?

I never think whether they are male or female. I scale it according to how I rate the instructor. If they are good teachers I will be more serious about the criticism, and I'll regard it a little higher than if I don't care for the instructor. I just never think about whether they are male or female.

Do you think women artists work out of a different context than men?

A really interesting example of that is in our fashion design course. Our female instructor will let us use more ruffles, and encourages us to create more provocative clothing, but our male instructor doesn't encourage us to do that. It's interesting, but in this case they're both working out of their own attitudes, I guess. Our female teacher thinks it's OK to be sexy, but not our male instructor. He wouldn't care anyway, because he doesn't seem to be interested that way in women. So like, you know, he prefers women in tailored suits.

I never really thought about creating from a biased attitude, but come to think of it, that's true. I just never thought about it, but maybe now I will.

I think women have a tendency to use a lot of circles and organic forms in their work, but then so do men sometimes. Oh well, maybe there are two kinds of visions. Here, I really see a lot of circles—like my final project has circles in it. Another girl though, in my class, paints all hard-edge stuff, so I don't know. Maybe there are two completely different ways of working, but it seems to me the big stuff, the hard-edge stuff that you see in the galleries is what is more important. It's like getting back to the whole craft versus fine art business again. There can exist two things, but one always seems to be given more importance than the other.

I remember a few years ago. There was a big scene about doing anything phallic. The students were told by the head of the curriculum department that they were not allowed to do that.

Do what? I don't understand.

In sculpture. It happened to my roommate. She was a sculpture major, and a senior. One day she was down in the sculpture room and there was a bunch of alumnae, a bunch of old ladies, and she was sitting down there working on a wooden penis, and they became very upset, and it got back to the curriculum department head, and he notified the sculpture department that the students were not allowed to do such sculpture any more, or anything like it.

Isn't that curious? Men have always been allowed to use women's bodies as inspiration for art forms. We certainly have seen enough paintings of our breasts and other choice pieces of our anatomy used as inspiration . . . .

Yeah, using a female nude is OK but anything like using a male as the object in a drawing or sculpture is out.

One of the biggest insults a male instructor can give you is to tell you to quit and go get married.

You have a large professional gallery here at the college. How many exhibits have you seen there that were women's work?

Alice Neel was the only woman I can remember.

Does that include all of you?

Yes.

Most of the exhibits have been always by male artists.

At an all-women's college, what role models do you have? Whom do you admire in the art field?

For me, it's the professionals in the field. I don't think of them as black, Chinese, women or whatever. I just look at their work.

When you have a life model, is he completely nude? There was a time when women were not even permitted into a life-drawing class. We never saw the totally naked man, although the women models were completely nude.

That's really an interesting question, because it was only last year that the model was completely nude here, the male model that is.

No wonder women artists have never created a "David." The damn model would never take off his pants.

Do you have more female models or male? I know the department head is a male, and I was curious.

It's about fifty-fifty.

Do you feel as students you are being encouraged to develop your own voice and style?

It's really funny, I think a few of us might have by now, because we are seniors. We *should* have developed our own style, that is, but in a way our instructors kind of make a joke out of it, not maliciously of course, but remarks like: "What a pity you can be identified," and saying, "Well, if your work is so recognizable it can get boring." They tell us we should be diversified.

Why do you think by the time you are seniors and have been through the various disciplines that you haven't developed your own personal way of seeing? Is there fear that women expressing a totally different vision than the accepted one could reflect back on the school? Because the manner in which our society treats women, or values our artistic vision, the school is "protecting" itself against letting the world know this is a school for women. Women should have their own vision, working as they do out of a completely different context than men, not because of their sexual heritage, but because society has conditioned women to accept certain stereotyped concepts. Men too have been conditioned, but society itself has been conditioned to believe that all art is to be judged from a masculine perspective. Wouldn't it be safer then to train women art students to create from the male-oriented vision, or encourage them to become androgynous in their style so that no one will suspect that they are working from a different context? Naturally, I don't believe that this will ever be a conscious direction or subversive plot, but I do believe that it exists unconsciously. In both cases, whether creating from a male perspective or encouraging androgyny, we are castrating women's vision in order to direct their work toward a stereotype of what the art world considers 'good' art. I would like to wish you success as women artists, and to encourage you to have the strength to pursue your own personal visions as women, regardless of how painful at times that might be.

The following brief interview is with a female artist/instructor and also a graduate of this small women's art college.

How would you describe your work currently?

I do work very similar to what I teach. I'm doing color-field painting and the relation of one color against another. I did that for about five or ten years. Now I'm investigating black and white and the use of neutrals and line to depict form using neutralized color with black and white line.

I've been lucky in getting it into shows. I got one of them into a show that was judged by the curator of the Whitney this year, and then I got another prize on a similar work. So what I'm trying to say is not that I got in and got a prize, but that they are successful, they are working.

What or whom do you feel has been the strongest influence on your work?

I've answered that in part, since I'm doing what I teach. How can you live with something all day and then go home and do something entirely different? That is what I was doing some years ago. Originally I was a very realistic painter. When I came here years ago to teach, I did watercolor in a very realistic way, and then when I got to the point where I could knock out watercolors in nothing flat, it became no challenge—you've got to do something else, to go somewhere else, and so where do you go? You go where everyone else goes, into less and less, and more and more minimally, and then arrive at a point and work within that. So if I had to say one *artist* influenced me, I'd have to say no. But I think the *person* who was the greatest influence on me, forever and ever, was my high school art teacher. I could not have done anything without him. He came to the college and talked them into giving me a scholarship, because we had absolutely no money or anything when I was a kid.

And here you are now, an instructor, a full professor, in the very place where you studied as a student . . .

Yes, that is part of the reason I feel such an empathy with the kids that are here. I've been through it myself. Besides that, I owe this man the biggest debt. He was a fantastic guy. At one time the art editors of all four big magazines were a product of this man—he was their art teacher too. They all came out of this one guy—what a teacher.

Then he did more to encourage and influence you intellectually, he gave you more self-confidence . . .

Yes, that's right, he really encouraged me as an individual.

How would you define female imagery? How would you define working from the female experience?

Well, I know there are people who think there is such a thing as *female* imagery. I don't. I think there is *human* imagery. I don't think there is such a thing as a *female* experience. We had a discussion here at the college the other day, and some people were saying that female imagery is a contained thing, a uterus, or a womb, that kind of business. I think that is a lot of hogwash.

You seem to feel very strongly about it.

Yes, yes I do.

Do you think your work reflects you as a woman?

No! I don't think anyone would know who did it if they looked at it. Years ago when I was an art student, which was ages ago, I did a poster that won first prize, and the big thing was the judge said to me: "Oh! it is so strong, it looks like a man did it." I thought that was terrible, really, I wasn't flattered at all by that statement. I was highly insulted.

Do you think that is because of the change of consciousness on your part? Are you reflecting back on it, or were you insulted at the time it was said?

No, I didn't like it when it was said.

Do you see things changing here or have attitudes towards women stayed relatively the same?

Well, things are changing, I guess, but you know . . . I've never worked in any place, that is, taught in any other place, where I've been other than the only woman. So, I think it's what you get used to.

Her adamant refusal to acknowledge a female vision or female imagery, and her constant reminders to me of her awards and acceptance is indeed interesting. She states that she would be "highly insulted" if anyone referred to her work as "it looks like a man did it," yet she refuses to acknowledge that her work reflects herself as a woman, and feels very strongly about this point. In reviewing her work, she is correct in her estimation—her work does not look like a man did it, nor does it look like a woman did it; it is safely androgynous.

Feminist Art Programs

There are two different choices in starting a feminist art program—within the community, or within an institution such as a school, college or university. Probably the easiest place to start a feminist art program is in the community, on a localized base. A grass roots group, as it were, will soon mushroom into a larger group as more and more people learn about the program and become interested. The word will soon spread concerning your intentions. Women who come together to draw and create, as well as talk about and reinforce each others' experiences, can be described as a "feminist" art group.

Most adult education classes are usually held in the evenings. This was one of the first concerns we faced in organizing a feminist art program, for we found that many women could not possibly meet during evening hours. Most women were exhausted at the end of the day, and creative efforts were the last thing they care to become involved in after caring for children, shopping, meal planning, etc. Our first concern then was arranging the program during the morning hours when most women would be alert, and would have their children either in school or nursery. Since most par-

ticipants were women, we felt we owed them this consideration. So, the sessions were arranged to meet twice a week
from 9:30 A.M. to 11:30 A.M. With the class ending at 11:30
A.M., the women then had time to get home for smaller children who might be returning from school.

We approached the continuing education division at the
local university and discussed our ideas concerning this program. We emphasized our concern in reaching women, giving women the opportunity to earn university credit without
the many hassles that accompany trying to attend evening
education classes. The administration was extremely interested in the idea of morning classes. Since the program
would be in affiliation with the local art association, we already had the facilities, and did not need space in the university, which, of course, would have presented a problem
for daytime continuing education classes which would be in
conflict with the resident program. The university agreed to
grant two credits for the drawing course, and also agreed to
pay "rent" to the art association for use of its facilities including easels and other equipment.

Our program was then easily established. The instructor
was approved by the resident art department chairman at the
university, and the first class met about four weeks later. It
must be pointed out that at no time did we stress a "feminist
art program." We were sensitive enough to realize the program would have lost all cooperation from the university at
that point, and we wanted very much to get it started first.
We were also aware that if the program sounded political we
would then lose many of the women we were trying to reach.
The women in the class, however, soon realized that this was
a different kind of drawing class. They found that they were
becoming aware of more things than the ability to be just
good drawing technicians.

We encouraged a great deal of discussion about their
lives, their problems. We also encouraged them to research
on their own any information concerning women's contributions in the arts. It should be pointed out that we also had

two or three retired men in the class, one of whom was a retired chairman of the theatre department at the local university. These men were sensitive and interested in the class, and eventually they became "feminists" themselves and our greatest supporters.

After about the second session, we no longer needed any advertising concerning the class. Word soon spread that something really fantastic was happening at the local art association. One woman in particular stands out in my mind. She had arrived, huge drawing board under her arm, and a rushed air about her as she moved across the room and grabbed an easel. She was an older woman, about sixty or so. She informed me that all her life she had devoted her time and energy to being a mother and hostess. Her husband had been one of the administrators at the university, and she found that most of her time had been playing the active role of hostess. "Now!" she said, "I intend to devote what time I have to myself. Don't ask me to "serve" on any committees, or to "join" anything. I'm here to paint, and I intend to go about it quite selfishly." Impressed with her spirit, but a little dubious about her declaration, I watched her as she returned to her huge luxury car to unload another batch of material. I was skeptical, for I had seen so many women in my classes who simply enrolled to pass time, women like her, wealthy, comfortable, and not particularly interested or serious about their art.

In only three sessions, however, this woman proved to be the most energetic, creative, and talented woman in the class. Her work was stunning. Her draftsmanship was fantastic. Her sensitivity and feeling concerning her own work, and other women's work was a joy. She continued through the full session and when the classes were over, she formed a group of women who continued to meet and paint each week from a model (usually male). Her dedication was so intense, that in spite of her "late" start, she has continued to have major exhibitions at various universities throughout the state, and her work is now represented in many private collections.

"Ms." pastel by Shirley Buell Bernreuter, 1974.

This past year, well into her late sixties, she traveled alone, without her husband, and enrolled in a drawing workshop in New York. Shirley Buell Bernreuter became, as it were, a role model for many other women of her age, including many younger ones as well.

We continued to maintain a good relationship with the university and throughout the community. We were reaching women who ordinarily would not have joined our group if the title "feminist" had been attached to it. These very women who were afraid of the words "women's liberation" and "feminism," found to their amazement that not all "feminists" were single, lesbians, or tough. The married and conservative women in the group who considered themselves "feminist" were probably our greatest role models. Women found they could create from their own experiences as women, and that these experiences offered a wealth of material for painting and drawing inspiration. By reinforcing their experiences, we found that these people were becoming aware and participating in meaningful, creative experiences. No longer were they involved in just the "techniques" of drawing and painting—techniques that taught them how to become good technicians, but unable to express anything in their work.

An amusing anecdote concerning this program happened during a class session. The women decided they wanted a life model, and thought that since most models were always women, it would be interesting to use a male model. It had been years, I was sure since many of these women had been in art school. Indeed, many had never even attended a drawing class before or seen a nude model. The model arrived, stepped up unto the stand and started to slowly disrobe. I assumed that he would have on a leotard, for he was a dancer, and I had asked him to wear a leotard for I felt that it was better to "ease" into the life model since many of these women seemed to me to be extremely self-conscious. However, the model stripped down to his underwear, and kept on going. I looked around the room as thirty-five women sat

behind thirty-five drawing boards, none of them talking, or
looking either to their right or left. Immediately they started
to draw, and the model slowly, and to my horror, pulled his
leg up and around the back of his head, his genitals not two
feet away from a woman sitting at the base of the stand. The
room was totally quiet except for the scratching of some
thirty-five charcoal sticks.

Suddenly the outside door to the studio opened, and a
woman entered who happened to be a board member of the
art association, and a very conservative and politically active person. I watched her face as it changed expression, and
she quickly looked down at the floor as she moved towards
me. I smiled at her rather weakly, and the message passed
through my head, "This is it, this will finish us off." She actually had come to ask about enrolling in our course, she informed me. Looking at her closely, I tried to see the anger
and embarrassment that I was so sure she must be feeling at
that moment. Then to my amazement, she whispered in my
ear: "My God! That's the first naked man I've seen in my life
with the exception of my husband." The next day she was
there, drawing board already set in position before the male
model even arrived. I learned a great deal from this little incident. I learned that I too had a lot of stereotyped ideas about
women—simply because they dressed or assumed a facade
that typecast them, when in reality, they weren't at all like
what their appearances seemed to project. I stopped worry-
ing, and I also stopped being overprotective of them as well.

Since the program was successful through the community association and the continuing education, I decided it was
time to advertise ourselves as a "feminist art group." I
wanted approval from the university to start a "Women in
Art" program. The interest generated by this program was
my impetus. Before it could be listed as a continuing education course, however, I would need approval from the resident art department chairman at the university. The next
four weeks I devoted to developing a course proposal and
outline for a "Women in Art" program to be offered through

the resident art department at the university. I was informed by the continuing education administrator that if the program were approved, we could then offer it through continuing education. Excited and overconfident, I contacted the art department chairman for a meeting concerning the proposal.

I had written to various universities and colleges throughout the country that offered similar programs. I received much information and best wishes from many women associated with these various programs. Together with this material and my course and outline proposal I presented the idea to the art department chairman. He seemed to be interested, and informed me that he had been taught in a college course that women never achieve in the arts. He continued to say that he had seen actual charts and statistics confirming this. He never informed me whether or not he believed what he had been taught, but seemed interested enough in the women's program to suggest I present the proposal at the next faculty meeting.

The next faculty meeting was scheduled for the following week. I was nervous about the proposal, for I wasn't confident enough in myself and felt intimidated by many of the faculty, whom I knew were very anti-feminist. We managed to pass out the proposal and I was given the opportunity to discuss the program. The faculty decided to vote on it, and I was asked to leave the room until they arrived at a decision. Walking out of that room and into a corner of the outer office, I felt at that moment like a school child being reprimanded for some petty crime. After what seemed like an eternity I was asked to return and was told by the art department chairman the proposal was being "put into committee." Those familiar with administrative techniques will realize this is a death warrant for any proposal or idea. In committee, our "Women and Art" could remain for any amount of time, safely "out of the way."

I think that at that moment I realized that women were still firmly outside the university system. Although the universities have been open to us, and that of course has only been within the last century, we are still not part of the system. We have been given the options to enter and study, but are frustrated if we try to make those options relevant to women. We have been allowed to join the male preserve, the university structure, but only if we think, act and study from their point of view. How simplistic and beautiful our women's program had been compared to the many frustrations and problems thrown in its way because we were foolish enough to think it would be understood and welcomed at this male bastion.

The committee chosen by the department chairman to review the "Women in Art" proposal was comprised of two women and myself, and two male faculty members. We met each week, every morning at 8:30 A.M. over coffee. Only the two female faculty members ever showed up at any of the meetings. In the meantime, I received a memorandum from another department notifying various faculty that a "Women in Creativity" course was being proposed for consideration. Concerned that our "Women in Art" proposal would never be considered or make it through committee, I notified the coordinator of this new proposal of my interest.

In the meantime, the "Women in Art" proposal was presented to the faculty without my knowledge, and was unanimously approved by the faculty. The art department chairman later informed me, rather casually, that the proposal had received favorable reaction, but now it would have to wait until he could obtain funding. He told me not to mention it to anyone, that he was working on several plans and wanted the "Women in Art" to be part of these plans. I believed him. It was only later that I was told he never followed through with the proposal; the proper papers and procedure for applying for a new course were never given to me by the chairman.

"Women in Art" died a quiet death. Its only effect, one enlightened and perhaps more aware woman. I learned a great deal from the experience, and decided I would use all the material from this course proposal to give assistance to

"Hari's Repose," pastel by Shirley Buell Bernreuter, 1975.

the newly forming "Women in Creativity" course which
looked as though it would be successful. The coordinator of
it was an English instructor. Her husband was chairman of
one of the larger fund-granting institutes at the university. I
knew, in this instance, money, or the excuse for lack of
money, would not be a consideration.

Interestingly enough, the chairman of the department of
art asked me if I would serve on this "Women and Creativity" steering committee representing the art department. It
should be remembered that I was not an appointed member
of his faculty, but was, in fact, only a teacher through continuing education, although I needed his approval as chairman of the department of art to retain even this job.

For the next six months I attended meetings representing
the art department. Also serving were women faculty members from various departments throughout the college, all
appointed, all salaried and compensated for their time. It
was an exciting six months. The women on the committee

were interested in women, and especially women's contributions in each of their own disciplines. A great deal of dialogue and information concerning women and creativity took place, and I felt stimulated and enriched by the experience. For the course, we decided to invite outstanding women as lecturers in our fields: theatre, music, English, French, psychology, art and art education. A list was drawn up using the names of outstanding women in all the above fields, and one name was chosen from each discipline. This woman would then be invited to lecture or demonstrate her craft through exhibitions or whatever. The students enrolled in the course would receive three university credits. Grades would be based on two term papers.

Earlier in the year I had attended a panel discussion at Moore College of Art in Philadelphia concerning women in the media. There I had met Alice Neel, one of the greatest painters of our century. Her portraits are represented in major collections; she has had a major one-woman exhibition at the Whitney, and her portrait of Andy Warhol was purchased by them. In addition, she is an outspoken feminist.

I had been in touch with her before this conference to obtain an interview, but she had informed me that since Philadelphia was closer to my home than her studio in New York, perhaps we could meet in Philadelphia. Also attending the conference was the feminist art critic, Lucy Lippard. I had an opportunity to speak with both women, and later Lucy Lippard wrote a letter to me wishing us luck with the "Women in Art" program, stating, "I envy you the art program." She also said that she had tried to start a "Women in Art" program, but it had failed, as the administration had really given her a hard time. It was not stated in this way, but much more to the point. She also suggested we use women in our art program who were "actually doing things" to change things rather than just any woman in general.

These two women came to mind immediately then, when drawing up a list of outstanding women in the arts. Excited over the possibility of obtaining some of Alice Neel's paintings for an exhibit in the art department gallery, I contacted the chairman and requested the possibility of having a one-woman exhibit of her work. Answering politely, he informed me he had never heard of her, and that was that. Unfortunately he had not attended my lecture the previous year where I had devoted forty-five minutes within the lecture to the work of Neel, including slides of her paintings. Over one hundred students, faculty, and general public had attended, and afterwards came forward to express their enthusiasm. Later, this lecture was published in a national magazine. The art department chairman obviously hadn't read that either.

By the time the "Women and Creativity" program was approved, however, one year later, I was packing for London. My husband was on leave and preparing to do post-doctorate work at the University of London. I had been invited by the chairman of the department of art there to present a lecture and seminar on women and art. The art department chairman at London University, I found, was extremely interested in feminism. Stanislaw Frenkiel, chairman and artist, and his wife Anna, a medical doctor, soon became close friends as well as colleagues. As chairman of the art department, Frenkiel arranged a series of seminars for me on women and art which were attended by faculty as well as the students. I found, after a year of frustrations dealing with administrators and people who had so many hang-ups about the feminist movement, that it was a joy to meet and become friends with such interesting and sensitive human beings.

Meanwhile, back home, I knew the "Women and Creativity" program was beginning without me. I was happy in the knowledge that at last the university was becoming relevant for over one half the student population—namely its women students, and I felt confident I had given all I could to the program.

The following year, upon our return, I found the course had worked fairly well, although it wasn't being offered again that term. Some rumors connected with it concerned the women faculty themselves. It was mentioned that many complained they were not given enough time from their regular class duties to fully participate in the program. Other complaints concerned the many hours involved. I was also told that a male faculty member had taken credit for inviting Alice Neel. This really amused me, for I recalled that not one faculty member or department chairman had heard of her when I requested a one-woman exhibition of her work. I assumed all of this didn't matter anyway, for I had learned a great deal from the experience.

I continue to teach, and do independent research on women and the arts. Unlike years ago, however, when my feminism was a conscious effort, today I have internalized the female values; this value system and approach to teaching is second nature to me now. Hopefully, my students, both male and female, will benefit from this teaching approach, an approach that is no longer biased to either the "male vision" or totally the "female vision." My life is richer today, the pains and frustrations brought on by it all have etched deeply into my psyche and have enriched my life. Perhaps none of us can truly be artists until we have accumulated enough of these experiences. The feminist movement in this country has, indeed, changed my life.

Selected Bibliography

A Dictionary of Miniaturists, John Bradley. Burt Franklin Publishers.

A History of the World's Fair Columbian Exposition, edited by Rossiter and Johnson, Vol. 1, narrative. New York: D. Appleton and Co., 1897.

Ancestral Voices, Decoding Ancient Languages, James Norman. New York: Four Winds Press.

Angelica Kauffman, Her Life and Works, G.C. Williamson and Lady Victoria Manners. London: Bodley Head Ltd., 1924.

An Introduction to Ancient Philosophy, A.H. Armstrong. London: Metheun and Co. Ltd.

Art and Handicraft in the Women's Building, edited by Maude Howe Elliott. Paris and New York: Goupil and Co. Boussod, Valadon and Co. 1893.

Beyond Stonehenge, Gerald S. Hawkins. New York: Harper and Row.

Columbian Exposition, Art and Architecture, William Walton. George Barrie, 1893.

Dawn of the Gods, Jacquetta Hawkes. New York: Random House.

Dictionnaire, Peintres, Sculpteurs, Nouvelle Edition. E. Benezitt. Libraire Grund.

Encyclopedia of Painting. New York, Crown Publishers.

Great Houses of Britain, Nigel Nicolson. London, New York: Hamlyn Publishers, 1968.

Hebrew Myths, the Book of Genesis, Robert Graves, Raphael Pata.

I Ching, translated by James Legge.

I Ching, translated by Richard Wilhelm.

Landmarks of the World's Art, Andreas Lonmel. New York: McGraw-Hill.

Mythology, David Leeming. New York: *Newsweek Books.*

Painting throughout the 18th century, Terisio Pignotti. New York: *Newsweek Books.*

Sara Siddons, Portrait of an Actress, Roger Manvel. London: Heinemann.

The Architecture of England from Prehistoric to the Present Day, Doreen Yarwood. London: B.T. Batsford, 1967.

The First Sex, Elizabeth Gould Davis. New York: G.P. Putnam and Son, 1971.

The Royal Academy of Arts, a Complete Dictionary of Contributors. From 1769-1903, Algernon Graves. New York: Burt Franklin, Vol. 11.

We the Women, Career Firsts of the 19th Century America, Madeline B. Stern. Schulte Publishers, 1963.

Art News Annual, "Women as Sex Objects," Linda Nochlin and Thomas Hess. Vol. xxviii, 1972.

Through the Flower: My Struggle as a Woman Artist, Judy Chicago. New York: Doubleday, 1975.

EVERYWOMAN'S GUIDE SERIES

EVERYWOMAN'S GUIDE TO COLLEGE
Eileen Gray
176 pages $3.95

A logical, no-nonsense study of the emotional, financial and academic realities of the returning woman student of any age. It includes sections on how to finance yourself in school and a field-by-field employment outlook for the woman college graduate through 1980.

EVERYWOMAN'S GUIDE TO A NEW IMAGE
Peggy Granger
128 pages $3.95

This practical guide presents a range of new ideas - from bioenergetic analysis to I Ching to humanistic psychology - along with a series of interviews with women who have successfully translated these theories into practical and meaningful changes in their lives.

EVERYWOMAN'S GUIDE TO TIME MANAGEMENT
Donna Goldfein
128 pages $3.95

A back-to-basics, step-by-step program tailored for the woman —
homemaker or professional — who is bogged down by routine
and wants to take charge of her life. The reader will learn to
establish priorities, set time limits, schedule realistically, com-
municate effectively, simplify tasks, systematize, delegate, and
anticipate problems. "Practical...innovative."---*Booklist.*

EVERYWOMAN'S GUIDE TO TRAVEL
Donna Goldfein
128 pages $3.95

How to get all the excitement, glamour, freedom, relaxation,
pleasure, and privacy traveling can offer. The author shares
her years of travel experience in an indispensable guide that
will help both novice and seasoned traveler enjoy the special
sense of freedom and release from routine that traveling offers.
Special chapters deal with international and emergency travel.
"Everything a woman should know about getting the most out
of going places the easiest."---*Chicago Sun-Times.*

EVERYWOMAN'S GUIDE TO POLITICAL AWARENESS
Phyllis Butler and Dorothy Gray
128 pages $3.95

This is a fact-filled handbook for all women who want a positive
introduction to institutional and power politics. It reviews the political structure, types of activity (volunteer, political pro, candidate),
how to get involved, basic do's and don'ts, the running of a cam-
paign, and much more.

EVERYWOMAN'S GUIDE TO FINANCIAL INDEPENDENCE
Mavis Arthur Groza
144 pages $3.95

Rich or poor, single or married, every woman's questions about how
to handle finances are answered in this comprehensive money book.
It covers investing, budgeting, credit, insurance, estate planning,
saving and security, as well as the new credit laws and government
programs affecting the monetary concerns of women.

BOOKS OF RELATED INTEREST

In CONVERSATIONS: WORKING WOMEN TALK ABOUT DOING A "MAN'S JOB," Terry Wetherby conducts frank interviews with women who have succeeded in traditionally male occupations. Included are a biochemist with the Viking space project, Top Fuel race car driver Shirley Muldowney and twenty others.
288 pages, soft cover, $4.95

Six celebrated risk-takers are biographed by Antoinette May in DIFFERENT DRUMMERS: THEY DID WHAT THEY WANTED. None of these fascinating women was content merely to hear the faint tattoo of a different drummer — each was determined to own the drum!
160 pages, soft cover, $4.95

Far from being limited to women, the Equal Rights Amendment (ERA) will dramatically affect 100% of the population, both directly and indirectly. IMPACT ERA is the first and only book to predict ways in which the ERA will affect individual rights, employment, education, and domestic relations, both legally and socially. Edited by the California Commission on the Status of Women.
288 pages, soft cover, $4.95

In NEW POETS: WOMEN, Terry Wetherby has gathered a powerful collection of poetry by the best of the emerging women writers. Voices from the ghetto, suburbia, the country, the city: all are here, speaking out of a great variety of age and ethnic groups and educational levels.
160 pages, soft cover, $4.95

Dramatic true stories of women who helped shape the American West are recounted by Dorothy Gray in WOMEN OF THE WEST.
160 pages, soft cover, $5.95

THE WORLD OF EMILY HOWLAND: ODYSSEY OF A HUMANITARIAN by Judith Colucci Breault is an important historical biography of one of the nineteenth century's foremost but forgotten activists in human rights.
192 pages, soft cover, $5.95

Available at your local book or department store or directly from the publisher. To order by mail, send check or money order to:

Les Femmes Publishing
231 Adrian Road
Suite MPB
Millbrae, California 94030

Please include 50 cents for postage and handling. California residents add 6% tax.

DATE DUE